ALLEN COUNTY PUBLIC LIBRARY

ACPL ITEM
DISCARDED

SO-AUF-026

8.7.72

Planning Buildings
for
Handicapped Children

IVAN NELLIST A.R.I.B.A.

CHARLES C. THOMAS, PUBLISHER
SPRINGFIELD, ILLINOIS, U.S.A.

© 1970 Ivan Nellist

First published 1970

Charles C. Thomas · Publisher
Bannerstone House
301-327 East Lawrence Avenue,
Springfield, Illinois, U.S.A.

Published in the British Commonwealth of Nations
by Crosby Lockwood & Son, Ltd.

This book is protected by copyright. No part of it may by reproduced
in any manner without written permission from the publisher

Printed in Great Britain

FOR RUPERT

1703475

PREFACE

The intention of this book is to provide information helpful to designers and all who are concerned with environment for mentally handicapped children. It is written in the belief that buildings and the larger environment can both make a positive contribution to the wellbeing, education and development of these children.

It is not a design manual. The needs caused by mental handicap cannot be measured with the same precision as the needs of a wheelchair case. Some reference is made to the needs of physical handicap since this sometimes coincides, but the information given is brief since the subject of physical handicap is dealt with admirably and in detail elsewhere.

Standard solutions to the problems of mental handicap may well be undesirable. Needs vary according to the nature of the community and work is organised in different ways. Widely differing opinions are held as to the best environment to provide. Thus it is possible to describe the field, to indicate these solutions and those features which are found to work well and to suggest promising lines for further development but it is not possible to recommend any standard solution.

Occasionally, comments made in this book may seem to be obvious. No apology is offered for this, as such comments are made only because they have apparently not been obvious to the designers of existing buildings. Comment is also made on design features which should not be used — again because they have been used all too often.

There are many recent buildings which do not serve their purpose well — through lack of understanding of the needs, lack of imagination and lack of sympathy. Excellent studies have been made by the Ministry of Health (now the Department of Health and Social Security) and by the Department of Education and Science, but the buildings which are built are mostly designed by local Authorities who often lack specialised personnel and resources.

It is asking a great deal to expect the designer to conceive in detail what might be the needs, the thoughts and feelings of children of various ages having a diversity of types and degrees of mental handicap. Nevertheless, some understanding is necessary if the best environment is to be provided for them.

This book is written in the hope that it will help towards such an understanding.

ACKNOWLEDGMENTS

The author wishes to express his thanks and appreciation to all those who have given help, criticism, and advice at various times. This in no way implies that they necessarily agree with all or any of the opinions expressed in this book but grateful thanks are nevertheless due to them.

In particular, acknowledgment is made to:

Dr Rudolf Herz, F.R.I.B.A., Dr.Ing.

Mr B. W. East, F.R.I.B.A., Architect to the Board,
South West Metropolitan Regional Hospital Board.

Dr Roy Barnes
formerly Principal Medical Officer, Mental Health:
Buckinghamshire County Council.

Dr Fairlamb
formerly Chief Medical Officer, Mental Health; Kingston upon Hull.

Dr. G. O'Gorman
Borocourt Hospital, Nr. Reading.

Mr A. M. Morley, Director,
the Ravenswood Foundation.

Mr John Nicholls, A.R.I.B.A.

Mr G. W. Lee, General Secretary,
National Society for Mentally Handicapped Children.

Mr T. H. Margetts, S.R.N.
Chief Male Nurse, Church Hill House Hospital, Bracknell.

Mr Humphrey Wilson

CONTENTS

LIST OF PLANS AND DIAGRAMS

LIST OF PHOTOGRAPHS

C H A P T E R 1

Introduction—the problem

Until recently, little was known about the problems and needs of mentally handicapped children. In many quarters no distinction was made between the needs of children and of adult mental patients, and there was a marked tendency to pretend the problem did not exist at all. Parents often struggled on their own without the benefit of expert advice and without any real outside help, and not surprisingly the struggle left deep and lasting marks. The luckier parents were offered a place for their child in a general mental hospital, a place which they sometimes refused in the belief, probably correct, that home offered a better environment.

Thanks to the efforts of voluntary societies and of individuals as well as the Department of Health, the climate in regard to mental health is now much improved, and there is a steadily increasing national awareness not only of the problem which exists but of the various means which are being used to try and find a solution.

Mental handicap covers many different problems and can include such conditions as brain damage, deformation, mental retardation leading to over-slow development, emotional disturbance, lack of adequate mental capacity — to mention only a few.

All these troubles result in a child failing to develop in the normally accepted manner and at the normal rate of progress. Some, indeed, may never develop at all. There is a minority — fortunately very small — of pathetic cot cases, grotesquely mis-shapen and deformed, who are unable to move or to co-ordinate movements and who are frightening and repulsive to the average person. For this unfortunate minority there is still very little that can be done within the present level of knowledge. Even for the majority, those happier children who by comparison are almost normal, complete cure may still be a long way off.

Fortunately, most of the children are capable of development in some way, and given the right conditions and the right care and assistance some can make really remarkable progress. To do so however, they require a blend of expert medical attention and treatment, day to day care, and training and education at the hands of people who are sympathetic and understand something of their problems and their fears. Above all, they require love and individual care and attention.

Treatment of such children is a laborious process in which progress is slow and often non-existent and great credit is due to those who give their services — services which can only be provided by a devoted team of men and women combining various skills, knowledge and ideas. In turn, the team cannot operate effectively without good facilities and this book attempts to assess what is meant by good facilities.

One of the greatest difficulties to be encountered in doing so lies in the fact that the situation is constantly changing. The children often communicate badly or even fail to communicate at all. They are difficult to understand and assessment of the value of a building plan, a room, a feature, a fitting, or any other matter can only be determined by the results it gives. These results are tenuous in the extreme.

Knowledge is constantly being extended. New ideas are being tried out. The investigation of a particular facet of the total problem can lead to the posing of a different solution. Thus one of the greatest needs is for flexibility, permitting the widest possible range of use.

Guidance in published form has been laid down for some of the buildings used by mentally handicapped children but not for all of them. The best known guidance material is the Local Authority Building Note No. 4 for Junior Training Centres. This was published in 1963 and is shortly due for revision. Since it was the first official material on the subject it can only be regarded as tentative. Much knowledge has been gained in the field since this particular document was written. In addition, there are a number of Building Bulletins issued by the Department of Education and Science.

Meeting the need

The problem under consideration however is not the design or planning of a single building, but rather an examination of the various needs which arise, the types of building which might best serve those needs and in particular what may be the most effective total environment. Thus, buildings for the care of such children may be of various kinds, both residential and non-residential. They may provide only for very young children, for older children or for a group of varying ages and capacities.

The most effective total environment can only be described as an amalgam of that which has proved and is proving most effective in furthering the children's development towards the fullest possible participation in life and the greatest possible realisation of their own potential.

In considering solutions to the problem, due importance must also be given to the needs of the staff. Designers are sometimes so preoccupied with the needs of the children and the facilities which must be provided for them, that they pay far too little attention to the welfare of the staff. Cramped and gloomy staff rooms, inadequate working space, long lines of communication and lack of

2

interview rooms, are all common faults. There are instances in which the supervisor's room would make a good high-security prison cell.

Such conditions are not likely to induce sustained enthusiasm and effort by the staff, and without a happy and effective staff nothing can be achieved. Some writers have gone as far as saying that facilities for the staff are more important than facilities for the children, but such comparisons are not likely to produce any conclusion of real importance.

The term "child" is not always entirely clear when writing of the mentally handicapped, since some remain "children" all their lives. Buildings for mentally handicapped children are primarily for those between the ages of, say, four years and sixteen years, namely the ages usually associated with school days. Within this age range they may be accommodated in Nursery Units, Junior Training Schools (which are themselves roughly sub-divided into age groups), Special Units and possibly in certain other ways which will be examined later. There are instances of family groups working well, in which the older children tend the younger ones and seem to enjoy it and learn by it.

Occasionally it is suggested that the children should not be dealt with as a separate age group at all. This does not seem reasonable since the potential rate of development is greater in childhood and adolescence that at any other time. Normal children would make more progress in far shorter time during this period and it seems reasonable to assume that, with the right treatment and assistance, the same is likely to be true of mentally handicapped children.

If this is accepted then the activities which are carried on and the facilities which are provided will be of extreme importance. It would seem that there are two great surges forward, corresponding to physiological changes at about the ages of seven and fourteen — always assuming, of course, that the child is ever going to make appreciable progress at all. This can only be a generalisation since, among mentally handicapped children, there is often a great difference in physical size, in behaviour and in apparent capacity between two children of identical age. The only certain comment is that physical age is a difficult yardstick and may be very misleading to the designer.

Design brief

It should be pointed out that the writer makes no claim to any medical or psychological knowledge and any comments bordering on these fields are made purely as a layman.

At the same time it is necessary for the architect and the designer to have some appreciation and understanding of specialist thinking in these fields if he is to collaborate fully and provide the best and most suitable facilities. The architect must therefore acquire knowledge by a study of the subject and by a personal study of children and their needs. Beyond this study he must learn by discussion with specialists, teachers, welfare workers and those in everyday contact with the children. Only in this way can he build up a picture of what is required, and begin to write the brief prior to undertaking planning and design. It is all too common to find that specialists, in common with other clients, are not particularly good at briefing the designer, and although they may complain bitterly about things they don't want (after they've got them) they rarely explain their exact requirement clearly and methodically. Thus the architect needs to build up his brief from rather confused and fragmentary data and must make his own study of the basic problem if he is to organise the brief correctly.

Characteristics of the children

For some years there has been a very awkward split between the fields of education and health; mentally handicapped children, already unfortunate, have been unlucky in not fitting neatly into either field. Care of the body is the concern of the health authorities whilst development of the mind comes under the heading of education. As a result the authorities have been divided as to who should look after such children, with very unhappy results.

Many of the children will not take a normal intelligence test or are incapable of carrying out I.Q. tests. Consequently it has not been possible to assess their capacity for benefiting from education. The fact that they have not carried out a test does not necessarily mean that they do not possess any intelligence; nor does it mean that they are not educable. In this, the authorities have simply failed to take cognisance of the fact that there is a small minority group where possible intelligence cannot be measured or encouraged by the normal means. Education has thus shown itself inflexible and as a result the care of such children has rested principally with the Department of Health and with local health authorities, though it is now becoming the responsibility of the Department of Education and Science.

Educationally subnormal children, namely those who are unusually dull or mildly retarded, receive full attention by the education authority but there is no easy way over the "frontier". In fact it is doubtful whether many of the fully handicapped children would progress to an E.S.N. (educationally subnormal) School in any case, and it seems far preferable that education should extend its scope and range to devise an entirely new set of criteria and possibly a new approach for these children.

Education authorities are undoubtedly taking an increasing interest in this field, an interest which is actively welcomed by parents. This in no way detracts from the wonderful work which has been done by health authorities in recent years. Since the emphasis must be on the development of the child it may be that a recently conceived combination of doctor, psychiatrist, and educationalist may together produce the maximum beneficial effect.

Geographical and social distribution

The geographical distribution of the children presents a considerable problem in itself. Numerically there are far too many such children but they are

4

distributed quite evenly among the population. As a result, they are scattered widely and thinly over much of the country with a corresponding increase in numbers where the population is densest. Even in cities the children are scattered over wide areas. As a result it is difficult to determine the most suitable and central point at which to provide facilities for them and there are considerable organisational problems involved in collecting a sufficiently large group to justify the provision of facilities. The problem becomes even more acute in sparsely populated country districts and there may well be a strong argument for the provision of more residential facilities, though this solution is not necessarily a good one for smaller children. The problem is examined in more detail in a later chapter, in which the various types of building solution are considered.

Social distribution does not appear to show any pattern of real significance. Statistics are fragmentary, but such data as exists suggests that distribution is reasonably even throughout various social and occupational groups. There are one or two minor exceptions to this. For example, autistic children as a group seem to occur more frequently in marriages in business/professional and academic circles. There seems to be little other evidence in favour of any particular social "weighting" and it does not appear that any specific conclusions can be drawn. Mental handicap also occurs amongst the children of immigrant families, and again the proportion and distribution seems to be about equal to that of the permanent population. Sadly, the problem appears to be one which is world-wide and shared by all races, although it does not receive equal attention.

Social reaction

Social reaction to mental handicap has improved a good deal and this is particularly true where children are concerned. The public still tends to find adults both embarrassing and difficult but mentally handicapped children are now much more acceptable than was the case a few years ago. In well-to-do society such children were often found a place in a private "home" and any further reference to them was both infrequent and discreet. The not-so-well-to-do regarded such a child as yet another burden to be borne, not always with very good grace, and they were left to struggle along as best they could, sometimes with more cuffs than care from the rest of the family.

Fortunately there has been a big increase in understanding and sympathy and the children stand a considerably better chance of improving than they have ever had in the past. All sections of the community are now convinced that more can and should be done, though there is still a long road to travel before it can truthfully be said that everything possible has been done.

One of the biggest problems is the very wide range of ability and capacity to learn, which results in each child needing careful assessment and detailed personal attention. This is true not only of the different broad groupings of mental handicap, each of which has its own characteristics and its own capabilities, but also of different children within the same group.

Types of handicap

In strictly non-medical terms the broad classifications likely to be encountered are as follows:

Mongols—These make up a large proportion of the total number of children subject to mental handicap. They are easily recognisable by distinct physical characteristics which lead them to be thick necked, chesty, often slightly puffy in the face and otherwise slightly "swollen" in appearance. They find speech difficult, especially pronunciation of words. They can vary widely in intelligence and ability and, in many respects, are fully aware of their surroundings and anxious to co-operate.

Autistics—In a sense they are the very opposite of mongols. Relatively few in number they usually look perfectly normal and are often very good looking children. They are "withdrawn" however, often totally so, and appear to live in a world of their own. Frequently they do not talk at all and seem to take no interest in group play. They are often repetitive and obsessive in small actions. They are believed to be intelligent but through lack of interest and communication it is very difficult to "get through" to them.

Hyperactive children—A condition which may be combined with some other handicap. Again such children are prone to obsessive, repetitive behaviour, often of a noisy or violent kind (although the violence is incidental and not malicious). The children are emotionally disturbed and very tense.

Cerebral palsy—In this handicap there is a lack of physical muscular co-ordination. This is often akin to actual physical handicap. Jerky uncontrolled movement leads to frustration and emotional problems and the children are often unable to develop their intelligence fully as a result.

Schizophrenia—This is often described as "split personality" and as such it has been luridly over-dramatised by the public.

It leads to confusion in the mind as to what is "real" (in normally accepted terms) and what is not real and is accompanied by unreasoning fears which the average person finds difficult to comprehend.

Subnormality—This is a general term and the handicaps already described all share a degree of subnormality.

Subnormality is usually divided in this country into three degrees—slight, mild, and severe.

The severely subnormal are often hospital cases. Slight subnormality, in which the child is either not intelligent enough to attend normal school or is abnormally slow in developing, may lead to behaviour problems and emotional problems.

Mild subnormality is a border case in which the child may be able to progress or may need hospital treatment as he or she grows older.

Other Handicaps—Children may also suffer from other handicaps often physical, such as a physical deformity, blindness, partial sight, or deafness. These often combine with an emotional disturbance or even with actual mental handicap.

It must be borne in mind that these broad classifications are described in strictly lay terms. They are capable of combination and are also susceptible to degrees, so that, for example, it is possible for a child to be mildly autistic or completely withdrawn.

Aims in education

From the foregoing it will be seen that the children pose a variety of difficult individual problems. The solution to these problems is far from clear. Conventional education or anything resembling it is largely useless. Equally, however, it is a mistake to concentrate solely on the inculcation of acceptable social habits which, however well taught, can only equate the child to a performing animal. The ultimate aim must be to produce a balanced person able to exercise his or her mind and capable of further development in what would appear to be the most hopeful direction.

To achieve this the child must have an awareness, interest and the ability to communicate. This must be backed up by confidence in others and confidence in himself.

Furthermore, he must also be acceptable to society. The habits and behaviour of many of these children are often very anti-social. This may be due to lack of awareness, lack of interest, feeling of insufficiency or actual rejection. Whatever the causes may be, communication with the child is vital as a first step.

Love and the finding of a personal identity are equally vital. Communication can then lead to assessment, to social training, to activity training, to education, to the fullest possible development. The problem facing the designer is to determine what facilities are needed, what environment and what kind of buildings and surroundings can best help in this grand design.

CHAPTER 2

Solutions, types of buildings,
general considerations

It would be absurd to pretend that buildings can do much towards solving the problem of mental handicap. They can, however, provide the facilities and the environment in which doctors and teachers can grapple with the problem.

As yet there is no full solution in a medical or an educational sense, so the solving of the planning problem posed by the needs of doctors, teachers and the children themselves must likewise be tentative.

A planning solution which works well in one district may not be equally satisfactory in another. Many factors are likely to influence the siting and design of the buildings: some of the most important of these are:

1. The size of the local health authority and its independence or inter-dependence with other neighbouring authorities. This will determine the extent to which individual buildings and groups of buildings can be planned to fulfil specific functions. In the smaller and less wealthy authorities it may be that one building will have to combine a number of functions, though such a building if carefully designed may not necessarily be any less effective.
2. The "catchment area" which the buildings are intended to serve and the approximate proportions in which various kinds of mental handicap are estimated to exist. It should be remembered that conditions are seldom static but change quite frequently.
3. The opinions of the local medical officer of health and officers for mental health as to what is required and also the ability of these officers to convince their committees and obtain the necessary sanctions, together with the agreement of national authorities such as the Department of Health.

Assuming that this has been dealt with successfully, the design and planning of the building then becomes a matter for continuing discussion and collaboration between the medical officers, psychiatrists, welfare officers and architects.

A formal briefing in which the type of accommodation required is stated and the matter then left to the designer is no use whatever when devising buildings of this type. There must be a constant, close, and sympathetic collaboration between all the experts concerned and this cannot be emphasised too strongly.

4. Differences in total numbers to be accommodated are likely to have a marked effect on the building.

5. Regional and local differences must be taken into account. There are differences between town and country and between one part of the country and another which may have a bearing on the design. In most respects the buildings should relate to "home" atmosphere and the characteristics and way of life which denote home are therefore important. It will thus be seen that at any given point, solutions are likely to vary considerably.

The opinion has been expressed by some medical officers that what is needed is just space — the maximum possible space with the greatest possible flexibility in its arrangement so that it can be sub-divided and re-grouped as often as seems appropriate. This is an over-simplification. Even so, there is such tremendous variation in mentally handicapped children, both as regards behaviour, capabilities, age, and size that almost none of the normal school criteria can be applied. Thus, constant change and constant experiment are needed and these clearly demand maximum potential for detailed flexibility in the building.

In this context a clearly defined cellular plan with rigidly defined boundaries formed by solid partitions similar to those in a normal school is not the answer, though a building in which nothing is clearly defined and everything is constantly changing may be very disturbing to the children.

It seems therefore that maximum flexibility in use must be coupled with an appearance of stability and security.

Diagnosis

There are differences of opinion medically as to what can be done and what should be done for the children.

Generally speaking, diagnosis must come first. There are a few centres in the country, attached to hospitals for the most part, which are specifically diagnostic. The child stays at these for a short time—anything from two weeks to six months—and during this time he or she is observed methodically and tests are carried out to determine the nature and degree of the handicap and if possible the most suitable course of action to be taken.

Not all children are diagnosed in this way and it might be considered that the system is somewhat artificial and un-settling to the child. In addition, some handicapped children are remarkably intelligent in their own particular way and may put on a dramatic act if diagnostic processes are too lengthy and too obvious.

Points in favour of the system, of course, are the methodical and repeated observation and the opportunities offered for employing physiotherapy and speech therapy to test the child's physical capabilities. Hasty diagnosis may lead to a child getting either an incorrect or only partially correct "label" and once this label is attached it is almost bound to lead to a particular and pre-determined course of action, both medical, social, and especially administrative, which doctors and parents may regret at a later stage.

Quite often the remark is made that "Danny should never be at this Centre" or that "Susan has no need to be in Special Care". Unfortunately it is not always easy to make the necessary changes once a place has been allocated and those in direct contact with Danny or Susan may have to make the best of a bad job for some considerable time.

There are in fact two aspects of the problem, one being diagnosis, care and treatment for the child; the other being relief for the parents. The medical authorities are very much aware of the strain which a mentally handicapped child causes on the rest of the family. The mother is likely to suffer most but there is also a considerable impact on the whole family and on family life. The majority of parents have to live with the problem for as long as they can, but sooner or later they approach breaking point.

There is thus a constant need both for more facilities and for better facilities so that parents can have their children in day care and gain sorely needed relief.

The other and predominant aspect of the problem is that of treatment for the child. This ranges from medical treatment and straightforward "care", through various kinds of social training to a sort of rudimentary education.

Many of the children like to be able to do something useful and for the most part both training and education aim at the fullest possible development enabling the children to take a proper place in society, accepted with both their capabilities and their limitations.

Some of the children co-operate willingly but some are extremely difficult and uncooperative. Sometimes a change in environment and activities may establish a break-through and gain the child's interest and co-operation. Even the term "child" is somewhat fluid, it should be remembered that some are still "children" well after the age of adulthood.

Classification is thus difficult and buildings necessarily cover a very wide range of activities. Nevertheless there are certain clearly defined types of building which are intended to cover certain broad but recurring classifications.

Junior training schools

These constitute the best known type of building for the care of the children. They are the subject of a Local Authority Building Note (No. 4) which lays down in broad terms a certain amount of guidance material and which has been much used by local authorities in the design of such centres. In general, points concerning the function, size, siting, general design approach, suggested accommodation, services and equipment, as well as cost allowances for the building are covered.

This document was issued in 1963 and is now considerably behind current thinking in many respects, but the more general aspects of the document are still worthy of study.

Junior Training Schools have in fact been built for two decades and in the early days their planning and design were largely matters of conjecture. It is easy to criticise some of the earlier buildings, especially in the light of the knowledge we now possess, but it must be remembered that architects and medical experts who worked together in producing environment and buildings at that time had no guidance material and were intuitively developing what they believed to be best.

A Junior Training School admits children between the ages of three and sixteen. This does not necessarily mean that all handicapped children begin at the School at the age of three and remain until they are sixteen. In practice there is a very large "turnover". Some stay the full time but many enter at later stages, as places become available, or as they are satisfactorily diagnosed, or are switched from some other form of treatment, or when parents finally decide they can no longer manage alone. A certain amount of trial and experiment take place and children may also be switched to a different type of treatment, such as Special Care, hospital or E.S.N. School as and when advisors think this appropriate and a vacancy occurs.

The number at a centre is likely to be anything from sixty in a small centre to a hundred and thirty in a large one.

The Building Note lays down smaller, lower, and upper limits (thirty to a hundred and five) and expresses the opinion that a large centre is more able to

1. JUNIOR TRAINING CENTRE (NOW SCHOOL)—SUTTON, HULL.
One of the earlier Centres built in 1952.
Architect: Andrew Rankine, A.R.I.B.A., City Architect (dec'd).

2. A JUNIOR TRAINING SCHOOL, NORTHENDEN, MANCHESTER.
Built in 1964
S. G. Besant Roberts, F.R.I.B.A., City Architect.

divide the children into suitably classified groups for training. It also has obvious administrative and financial advantages though there may be a danger of losing something of the domestic scale and perhaps also the personal attention. "Classes" are divided loosely into nursery, junior and senior, and there may be two or three of each. These, however, are not divided according to age but rather according to ability, so that there are likely to be two or perhaps three junior groups undertaking work at different levels in which the children are all of mixed

ages. The only modification that would be made is when, for example, a child who is still an infant in outlook becomes too old and physically too large to be accommodated any longer in the nursery group; he or she would then be transferred to the juniors although the necessary mental progress would not have been achieved.

An important point about Junior Training Schools however, is that the children in them are mostly trainable and a real "problem case", if correctly diagnosed at the proper time, would be placed in a Special Care Unit.

Classes are mixed and usually consist of between fifteen and twenty children and a staff ratio of one to ten is considered good. In fact, staff illness and similar problems often increase this figure and it is sometimes necessary to combine two classes.

As a general observation, the children need as much individual and personal attention as possible and, depending on the nature of their handicap, they often only make real progress when they receive such personal tuition. Administratively and financially this is difficult, and if a child is able to receive ten to twenty minutes personal tuition a day he is doing well.

The children attend on a day-time basis, keeping the same times and having the same breaks and holidays as a normal school. They arrive by coach or minibus which collects them from various established picking-up points and they stay at the School for the mid-day meal.

They are likely to be suffering from a variety of mental handicaps in varying degrees and some may be physically handicapped as well.

Activities are varied. "Classes" are much less formal than in normal schools and consist more of groups sitting round in a circle. At the nursery stage, activity

3. NORTHENDEN CENTRE, MANCHESTER.
Another view showing approach from main entrance. Note the fence providing segregation of children from local road traffic approaching the centre.
S. G. Besant Roberts, F.R.I.B.A., City Architect.

is virtually all play, but a measure of organised discipline is worked into the day when children progress to the junior section. A good deal of activity centres on social training in its widest sense but elements of simple education are introduced for those able to profit from them.

Manual craft and art activities are much used, together with music and movement (most children develop a good sense of rhythm), physical games and training, dancing, household and domestic training.

The buildings are single-storey and usually on a fairly open site. Accommodation needed and its planning in detail is examined in a later chapter.

Transition for older children

At the moment the question of what happens to children when they reach the age of sixteen has not been conclusively resolved. The most logical step seems to be progress to an Adult Training Centre. Alternatively, they may move to a residential hostel, and work in a sheltered workshop, they may enter a hospital or they may even return home and carry out fairly simple jobs. Whatever the solution, the step is an important one. The change from school to employment is a major step in normal development and is proportionately greater for handicapped children.

There would seem to be an argument for a transitional class in which leavers spend a certain amount of time, before making a complete change. As yet it has not been resolved whether such a transitional class is best held at the Junior Training School or at the Adult Centre, though it seems arguable that the class should be held for part of the day at the J.T.S. with part-time attendance at the new Centre. It is well worth considering the placing of a group of buildings for Juniors and Adults in proximity to one another, since this enables the transition to be made as gently as possible.

Special care

No one has produced a clear definition of the nature and purpose of a special care unit and medical officers and authorities have differing views as to how it should be used.

Sometimes a special care unit exists entirely on its own, often it forms a part of a junior training centre and occasionally it is combined with other buildings. Basically, a special care unit is for those children who are unable to fit into the junior training pattern, either because they could not gain benefit by it or because they would disrupt the activities and distract the other children.

Many children in special care do not talk or communicate. Many of them have behaviour problems such as giving vent to sudden and uncontrolled noise or movement, aggressive or destructive tendencies, completely unpredictable actions, obsessive repetitive acts, and severe incontinence. Many are deeply disturbed emotionally.

Some have mental/physical handicaps such as brain damage and thus lack the equipment ever to improve very much.

Some local authorities put virtually all physically handicapped cases, both cot and wheelchair, into special care units. Thus, there are those who clearly can never be trained or educated and some who may possibly be educable to varying extent but have not been clearly diagnosed and a course determined. The range is very great and this is a strong argument for having a special care unit divided into a number of sections so that provision can be as varied as possible.

A small minority may be able to progress to a Junior Training School—which by comparison is a very reasonable and normal establishment!

Special Care Units are single-storey buildings with a large play area, both indoor and open air. Play is often messier than in the Junior Training School and the building a good deal noisier. Apart from this, facilities are similar but particular thought must be given to design, detailing and equipment for physically handicapped cases and for cot cases.

Toilet, washing, and laundry facilities are more ample and the number of children accommodated is smaller. Staff ratio is often higher. The children attend on a day-time basis as in the Junior Schools and travel by coach in the same way. Physically handicapped cases travel by ambulance.

Nursery units

These are usually sections forming part of a Junior Training School but are occasionally built as a separate unit in a manner similar to Special Care Units. They enable careful and systematic observation to take place at an early and formative age but whether thay are provided as a separate and self-contained facility will depend on local conditions and on the views of the local health authority.

4. NURSERY CARE HAS ITS OWN PARTICULAR PROBLEMS AT GLOUCESTER
Fully curtained windows and door between classroom and outdoor place space.
John R.Sketchley,A.R.I.B.A.,Dip.T.P.A.M.T.P.I.,City Architect. (Formerly J.V.Wall,A.R.I.B.A.)

Residential hostels

These are for older children and adults and provide full-time living facilities when their own home is either unsuitable or non-existent, or is too far away from medical/psychiatric care, training and employment. The residents have breakfast at the hostel, go out to work during the day, either in sheltered workshops or with local firms, and return in the evening for a meal, relaxation, games, television, reading, and of course to sleep. Some teenage children fit very readily into this pattern, but would soon lose confidence and deteriorate if they did not have the reassurance and supervision which the hostel provides.

Residential hostels may be limited to either all male or all female accommodation, and have a resident warden. The buildings are usually two-storey and as "homelike" as possible, with small dormitories, bedrooms, a lounge/games room, provision for quiet activities and for dining.

Hostels are often combined with Junior Training Schools and similar buildings. The interaction in such a case is good since there is shared interest and an easy transition as the children grow. An interesting combination has been tried in which a residential hostel was built at first-floor level over a Special Care Unit.

Residents use the kitchen and dining facilities for breakfast, go out for the day, during which time the younger children use the same facilities. At four o'clock the day-children leave and the older residents return. In practice it seems to work quite well and ensures that maximum use is made of the building and staff services, with resultant economy in running costs.

There are many combinations of hostel use. Some residents only use the hostel on a five-day week basis, returning home at the weekends. Some are permanent full-time residents and some are at the hostel on a short-term stay from time-to-time.

Sheltered workshops

These are not, strictly speaking, buildings connected with the care of mentally handicapped children, but are mentioned here since a few of the older children enter sheltered workshops at ages under sixteen. This happens when they seem unlikely to develop further at a School but show interest and aptitude in practical work. If the School does not have a practical room, or facilities are not sufficiently wide in scope, then the sheltered workshops may provide both therapy and occupation.

They are single-storey buildings providing workshop accommodation in which a wide variety of simple tasks can be carried out. Work consists of fabrication in timber, wire and light metal work, assembly, packing, the making of simple wiring assemblies, light electronic circuits — in fact virtually any type of work which is within the occupants' capabilities and for which there is a demand. Work is undertaken for local employers on a sub-contract basis with the approval of the unions and agreed rates are paid. Understandably, these are low since output and consistency are both rather uncertain.

The workshops are small in scale, airy and well lit and as flexible as possible in their arrangements to permit the undertaking of such a wide variety of tasks.

Educationally subnormal schools

These are midway between the Junior Training School and the normal school in their role activities and in the type of building. Sometimes they are loosely linked to a Junior Training School and this has been found beneficial to children and staff.

Hospital units

These are units for the care of children who apparently cannot respond to any of the other facilities already mentioned. Basically they are concerned only with the medical treatment and care of the children.

Non-ambulant (i.e. cot and bed cases) occupy small wards of normal design with an extension in the form of a day nursery, and outside play space for those who are able either to be moved or to walk by themselves.

Many of these are chronic, severe cases whose progress is restricted by the present limits of knowledge and treatment. All that can be given is physical care and attention.

Combined facilities

These consist of a complex or group of buildings on a large site, consisting of a Special Care Unit, Junior Training School, and Adult Centre, Hostel and Workshops or a combination of some of these. Taken together, they make transition between the various stages easier and permit greater flexibility in considering and testing the aptitude and capabilities of the children.

5. SHELTERED WORKSHOPS, BLETCHLEY, BUCKS.
F. B. Pooley, F.R.I.B.A., A.M.T.P.I., F.R.I.C.S., County Architect, Buckinghamshire County Council.

6. SCHOOL BUILDING FOR EDUCATIONALLY SUBNORMAL CHILDREN, GLOUCESTER.
Shows the relatively small scale and informality.
John R. Sketchley, A.R.I.B.A., Dip.T.P.A.M.T.P.I., City Architect. (Formerly J. V. Wall, A.R.I.B.A.)

7. ST. LAWRENCES SCHOOL, ST. LAWRENCES HOSPITAL, CATERHAM, SURREY.
A particularly good example of sympathetic siting.
Architect to the South West Metropolitan Regional Hospital Board. B. W. East, F.R.I.B.A. (Formerly Richard Mellor, F.R.I.B.A.)

20

CHAPTER 3

Overall Planning

Overall planning of buildings for the mentally handicapped is likely to be influenced by a number of factors which are not encountered elsewhere. Although there are different types of buildings providing facilities for the care of such children, it is possible to make a number of general comments regarding planning which will apply equally to the various types of buildings required.

Siting

Selection of a suitable site is very important, though it is appreciated that the designer is not always able to influence this. In some cases the Local Authority may already have a site reserved, but if the designer considers it unsuitable he should clearly say so.

At one time, because of adverse public opinion, sites had to be away from ordinary residential areas. There has always been a good deal of prejudice against the mentally handicapped and, to some extent, this still exists. Mental illness is feared, usually by those who have had no real contact with it. The mentally handicapped are stigmatised as "loonies", most probably violent, quite likely to be sex maniacs and prone to attacking passers-by. This is a hopelessly inaccurate picture, and nothing could be further from the truth.

On the other hand, mentally handicapped people, including children, do indulge in odd behaviour which makes people self-conscious and uncomfortable. Many do not want to be seen in close proximity to patients in case they are regarded as "odd" themselves.

There is also, of course, the old cry that the arrival within the community of a group of mentally handicapped children is going to "lower the tone of the neighbourhood"

Above all, people do not want to know about mental disturbance. Whether they want to know or not, however, it exists, and can only be combatted by understanding and acceptance. The work of voluntary organisations, such as the National Association for Mental Health and the National Society for Mentally

Handicapped Children, has helped greatly in giving more publicity and bringing about greater understanding and knowledge, both of the nature of the problem and of what can be done to help.

Once it has been accepted that this is a problem to be faced like any other, then there is a reasonable chance of attaining the co-operation between the community, the staff and the patients that is vital if any progress is to be made.

Many children suffering under mental handicap have a very real wish to be accepted and the siting of buildings for them within the living community is a matter of real importance and positive value.

If the children are to gain confidence, they must be not only in the community but *of* it—in a word, they must be accepted for themselves.

It should not be overlooked that buildings frequently need room for future expansion. For example, the number of children may be increased at a future date, extra and specialised facilities may be provided or the building may be extended by the provision of further specialised facilities in the light of experience gained.

Broadly speaking, the main siting possibilities are:

Centre partially attached to an existing hospital

This has advantages in the case of a residential centre for disturbed children. Staffing (which is a twenty-four hours a day matter), is made easier and medical care and supervision is readily at hand.

Catering can be arranged easily through the centralised hospital catering organisation.

Laundry, a problem which looms abnormally large in centres of this type, can also be arranged to advantage through the hospital's centralised plant.

There is a very flexible range of care possible, from the fully ambulant visiting "day-care" patient, to those cases needing a hospital bed and heavy sedation, and a ready interchange is possible between the various types of care and treatment.

A further advantage, from the planners point of view, is that hospitals frequently have land available within their precincts which can be used for such a building or group of buildings. However, it must again be stressed, that buildings for mentally handicapped children should never be more than loosely annexed to a hospital and should always look outward to the normal world, rather than inward to the hospital itself. Otherwise, there is a very real danger of becoming a close community in which the child, quite often protected by kindness and care, leads a sheltered life with no incentive to reach out to the world for himself.

Centre partially attached to an existing school group

Like the alternative above, this arrangement has advantages for the planner.

Land is often available either within the school precincts or nearby. Facilities such as playing fields and swimming baths can be shared. It has been suggested that there is also at least the possibility that children making progress in the

SITING

RELATIONSHIP OF BUILDINGS TO THE COMMUNITY

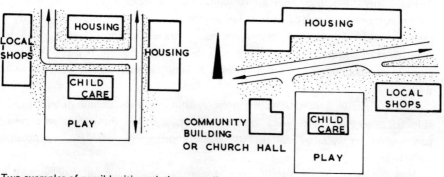

Two examples of possible siting relative to small neighbourhood communities with local (but not main) road traffic

Relationship of groups of buildings designed to give maximum continuity in care, education and training

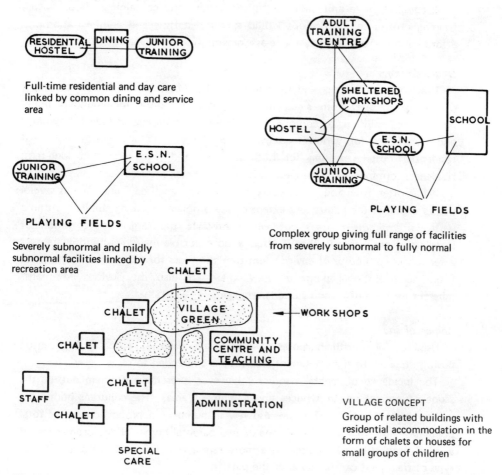

Full-time residential and day care linked by common dining and service area

Severely subnormal and mildly subnormal facilities linked by recreation area

Complex group giving full range of facilities from severely subnormal to fully normal

VILLAGE CONCEPT

Group of related buildings with residential accommodation in the form of chalets or houses for small groups of children

Fig. 1

Special Centre may be able to pick up the threads of education in the normal school. This argument however, is of rather doubtful value.

For many mentally handicapped children, the most that can be achieved within our present level of knowledge is that they can learn to communicate, to read and write in relatively simple terms, to travel, to shop, and to fend for themselves in society. They may learn to do a useful job which will give them a place in the community and self respect. A large number cannot aspire even to this.

In these circumstances, it seems unlikely that many such children will ever be able to take their place in a normal school, and for those few who might conceivably be able to do so, the dangers probably outweigh any possible advantage.

It is also worth noting that there is at least as much scope for improvement in the attitude of "normal" children towards mental handicap as in the attitude of their parents! One of the most promising combinations however, is that in which a Junior Training School is loosely linked with an E.S.N. School often with great benefit to both, as well as permitting great flexibility in assessment and placing.

A comprehensive unit based on village pattern and containing school, hostel, training centre, and workshops would simplify staffing and administration and afford continual opportunity for re-assessment and interchange.

Detached units

These account for a considerable number of the buildings which are provided, and range in size from small individual day-care units for young mentally handicapped children, to comprehensive groups of buildings including playrooms and classrooms for various age groups, sheltered worshops, youth club, and residential hostel, catering for both day-care and short-term and long-term residence, forming a very comprehensive and complex group of services.

It has often been found necessary to distribute small day-care units at several points owing to the nature and extent of the problem of young children within a particular catchment area, but where possible the larger concentration of buildings is preferable in that it offers a more flexible instrument and guarantees a far longer continuity of environment over the years for the children concerned. From an operational point of view, there are also the obvious advantages inherent in the staffing and running arrangements generally.

Choice of site

Usually, for health purposes, buildings are sited in a reasonably central position relative to the catchment area they are intended to serve.

The incidence of mental handicap, however, presents a problem outside the scope of normal health services and catchment areas. The childrens homes are widely scattered and as they are also few in number, in proportion to the total population, the removal of even one or two parental homes or the progression of a small proportion of children to a more senior establishment or to a different type of treatment centre can alter the pattern.

The main problem is one of transport and communications. Children attending special day units are collected by coach at various pick-up points, the coach following a circuitous route which may take an hour or more before the children finally arrive at school. There is thus a very strong argument in favour of considering the road pattern of the area before selecting a site, and if possible finding a site which is well placed in relation to main lines of communication. Supervision is needed during coach travel, and if children are handicapped to a degree where they are likely to fall out of their seats, they are unable to travel by coach at all.

In the case of long-stay residential units, the same problem does not arise and there is no particular reason for such buildings to be sited centrally, relative to the area which they serve.

The site should be well placed to share the life of the community. There is always the need to stimulate interest and awareness. As a corollary, it is valuable that people should be aware of the children and develop a knowledge and sympathy which will help to bridge the adequate and the currently inadequate.

Caution must be execised in choosing the level of outside activity which is to impinge on the centre. Intense, exciting, and noisy activity may not be good as a constant neighbour. For example, the nearness of a motorway, or a heavy industrial plant is unlikely to be beneficial, whereas a local community area, with secondary roads, a small local shopping centre and perhaps an active church with a good weekday programme could be of great value.

The site area required is not necessarily extensive. In addition to the buildings themselves, some open play space is needed, mainly grass, but the numbers of children involved are not large and in general it is preferable to have a small establishment in which the children can feel "at home". Within the limits of what is practicable from an organisational point of view, the smaller the group the better, with of course a high staff/child ratio.

This is not to say that the overall group of buildings is necessarily very small, but rather that each unit within the group should be small in scale and numbers, and designed to fulfil a particular function or line of approach.

It should be noted that official policy has sometimes been that units should be relatively large in order to give a full range of services and consequent flexibility, but this does not preclude dividing the overall group into units more intimate in feeling.

Area required

Buildings are usually single storey (with the exception of two storey residential hostels and a few central area buildings in cities) and require a generous horizontal spread with good, but not excessive, day-lighting. A typical special care unit on its own might require a site area of about 2 100-3 150 m^2 (½-¾ acre) as a rough guide.

A Junior Training School for eighty to one hundred children might need a site area of roughly 4 000 m^2 (1 acre) allowing for adequate outdoor space. A two

c

storey residential hostel for forty to fifty places would need a site area of roughly 1 000 m² (¼ acre).

Topographically, there are advantages to a site on a slight rise. A site on rising ground gives the advantage of a pleasant and open outlook even where surrounded by other buildings. A good site would be one having a gentle south or south-east slope with access from a road on the north or west.

A certain amount of reasonably level open space is needed for outdoor play, but slopes of up to one in ten can be utilised by means of judicious terracing and ramping and have resulted in very successful schemes.

One very real advantage of a sloping site is that safety and security precautions such as fences can be hidden very effectively.

CHAPTER 4

Activities

In order to devise the building fabric, it is first necessary to have a full understanding of the activities which are to be carried on.

It is doubtful whether buildings for the mentally handicapped are designed at the present day with such a full understanding. Many of them show evidence of having been designed with only a very superficial knowledge of proposed activities and without any genuine insight or sympathy for the occupants. As a result public money is wasted on buildings and equipment which do not function adequately or effectively.

Although at national level and in some of the regional hospital boards the design climate is constantly improving, this is not so at local authority level where resources and knowledge are both much less.

A less obvious pitfall lies in the undue weighting of the building towards the activities of a particular group. For example, in some cases the layout functions very efficiently for the smooth running of a programme of activities but lacks the personal and human family character needed for small children. Light airy rooms and spaces, modern colour schemes and even flowers on the window cills are not sufficient to disguise an "institutional" building. The institutional character must be completely removed. This is not easy since planning for a number of children must involve consideration of organisational problems and administration, and this in its turn is likely to lead to the design of a building which functions well from an administrative and staff point of view but expresses the mass-handling and "processing" of the children.

Such plans may arise from a lop-sided briefing to the architect, in which the administrative elements are represented too strongly, or from the architects own predilection for organisation. It should never be forgotten, however, that there are two sets of activities involved in all such buildings—those of the staff—and those of the children, and the building exists primarily for the benefit of the children! The whole building must be capable of use as a teaching instrument.

The activities of mentally handicapped children are likely to be varied and, by normal standards, unusual. Some children retreat into complete non-activity and

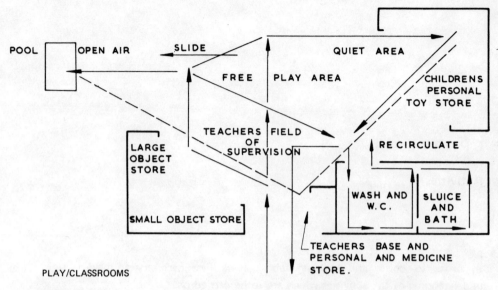

POOL OPEN AIR SLIDE QUIET AREA

CHILDRENS PERSONAL TOY STORE

FREE PLAY AREA

LARGE OBJECT STORE

TEACHERS FIELD OF SUPERVISION

RE CIRCULATE

SMALL OBJECT STORE

WASH AND W.C.

SLUICE AND BATH

TEACHERS BASE AND PERSONAL AND MEDICINE STORE.

PLAY/CLASSROOMS

Nursery level
Ages 4 to 7 approximately

NOTE: Entrance must be definite and unambiguous ·
The choice of areas and activities should also be clear ·
The diagrams are intended to illustrate activity paths and NOT the shape or size of rooms

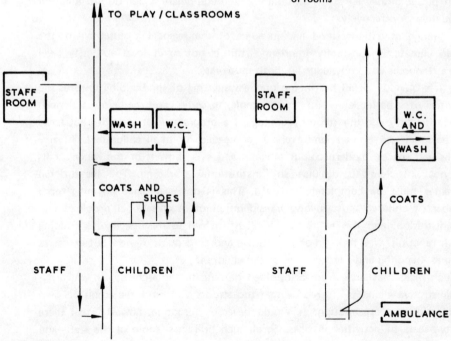

TO PLAY/CLASSROOMS

STAFF ROOM

WASH W.C.

COATS AND SHOES

STAFF   CHILDREN

ARRIVAL
AMBULANT CHILDREN
ALL AGES

STAFF ROOM

W.C. AND WASH

COATS

STAFF   CHILDREN

AMBULANCE

ARRIVAL
NON-AMBULANT CHILDREN (WHEEL CHAIR)
ALL AGES

ACTIVITY DIAGRAMS

Fig. 2

the aim in this case is to try and lead them back into acceptable forms of action. The designer planning a building for the mentally handicapped cannot take anything for granted and must question and re-assess all his normal attitudes and assumptions.

In most cases the over-riding aim is to persuade the child to become interested in normal attitudes and to acquire normal behaviour and outlook. The building and its facilities therefore must assist in every way possible.

Day training centres are becoming the largest category of building but whether the building is a day time Junior Training School, a Special Unit, a Residential Unit or other specialised building or combination of buildings, certain activities will be common to all. These activities are now examined in detail with reference to the rooms or spaces and facilities which are needed for their performance.

Firstly an examination is made of the general pattern of activity.

Day activities

Under the general heading of day-care units can be included Junior Training Schools, Special Care Units, E.S.N. Schools and all buildings in which a large proportion of the children attend only during the normal school working week and live at home. There may also be children attending who live in a residential hostel but this makes no difference to the pattern of daytime activity within the building.

The majority of the children will arrive by special bus or coach and each centre is likely to be served by two or three such coaches. A few may be brought to the centre individually by their parents, generally by car. It is unusual for the children to use public transport, principally because of the problem of supervision.

Each coach has a supervisor who sits near the door and receives the children at the various picking up points and keeps an eye on things generally. The coaches collect children from a large area usually in twos and threes at established points, so that the overall time involved may be anything up to an hour between the start of collection and final arrival at the Centre. Some of the children have thus had a long journey and it is hardly surprising if they get bored, though in general, handicapped children seem to enjoy riding in any form of vehicle and behave well. Potentially, there might be a case for varying the route so that the longer journey is shared by all the children at different times but the organisational problem and, in particular, the difficulty of establishing different picking up times with parents would be considerable.

The coaches usually arrive at the Centre not earlier than 9 a.m. and not later than 10 a.m. depending on local arrangements, which may vary slightly, and on the time of starting the journey. In general the periods and hours at which children attend are similar to those in a normal junior school.

On arrival the children are seen into the building by the supervisor, safely, except for the occasional "wanderer". A small number of children are confirmed wanderers and may drift away in the wrong direction if left unattended, or even take positive and carefully camouflaged steps to "escape". There is also the problem of the obsessive trait which compels a child to some activity such as touching the backs of all the seats in the coach. Patience on the part of the supervisor is not always rewarded, in that the ritual will be broken before it is complete and is repeated endlessly unless the child can be persuaded away. Such minor problems are an exception however, and most of the children disembark happily.

Age grouping

Age groups do not form the strong divisions apparent in a normal school. There are only three or four group divisions for purposes of the day's work. There are the nursery group, juniors, seniors, and special care — a term which usually embraces the particularly "difficult" cases. Sometimes streaming off into groups takes place inside the building by different circulation routes from the main entrance and sometimes it is achieved by separate entrances from outside. The latter planning solution works well in the case of the nursery group, especially where the small children are collected by a separate mini-coach or similar vehicle, but there seems little advantage in having separate entrances for juniors and seniors. Special Care is sometimes regarded as a special problem requiring a different building altogether.

Allocation of children to particular groups is a decision which rests with the Medical Officer, the Supervisor or Head, and the Mental Health Officer, and decisions will depend on a number of factors apart from age, such as standard of attainment and capabilities, behaviour and development. However, a child may be at last moved up into the next group, reluctantly, without noticeable improvement if he or she outgrows the group to an impossible degree.

Coats, shoes and toilet

Circulation from the entrance should be as simple and direct as possible. The first activity on arrival is the hanging of coats and the putting on of light shoes or slippers; a visit to the toilet follows. This is particularly necessary in view of the length of time some children may have spent in travelling. They are encouraged to wash their hands and move on to the classrooms. Some of the children will need not only encouragement but also a certain amount of assistance in these activities.

The whole process will require more supervision than is normally the case, though of course it is important for the children to become as self reliant as possible. Staff must be flexible in their treatment and move about amongst the children observing, giving assistance and encouragement and gently moving them on as seems needful.

Learning

Use of the term "classroom" is perhaps misleading since classes and academic activity are conceptions which do not fit well with the type of activity

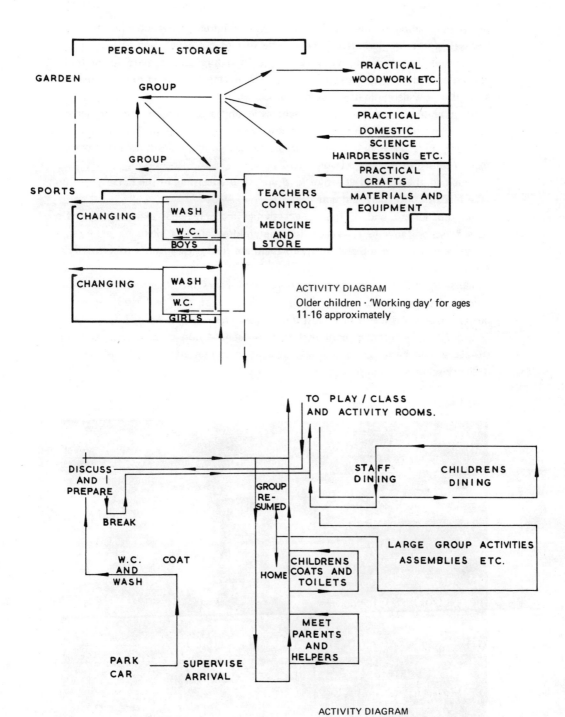

PERSONAL STORAGE

GARDEN

GROUP

GROUP

PRACTICAL
WOODWORK ETC.

PRACTICAL
DOMESTIC
SCIENCE
HAIRDRESSING ETC.

PRACTICAL
CRAFTS

MATERIALS AND
EQUIPMENT

SPORTS

CHANGING

WASH

W.C.

BOYS

TEACHERS
CONTROL

MEDICINE
AND
STORE

CHANGING

WASH

W.C.

GIRLS

ACTIVITY DIAGRAM
Older children · 'Working day' for ages
11-16 approximately

TO PLAY / CLASS
AND ACTIVITY ROOMS.

DISCUSS
AND
PREPARE

BREAK

GROUP
RE-
SUMED

STAFF
DINING

CHILDRENS
DINING

W.C.
AND
WASH

COAT

HOME

CHILDRENS
COATS AND
TOILETS

LARGE GROUP ACTIVITIES
ASSEMBLIES ETC.

PARK
CAR

SUPERVISE
ARRIVAL

MEET
PARENTS
AND
HELPERS

ACTIVITY DIAGRAM
Staff at day centre

Fig. 3

practicable amongst mentally handicapped children. It is possible to form "classes" for short periods in which some sort of group learning activity can be undertaken, but this will be very simple in nature and is more likely to be concerned with applied forms of learning. For example, learning to count may be applied to low denomination coins or groceries.

If a child is capable of real scholastic endeavour he or she will almost certainly be in a different type of school and not in a Junior Training School, although there are happy cases where a late developing child is able to move on from a centre to another school.

Much of the learning at senior level and all the learning in the nursery section take place through play and activities.

At the nursery end of the scale activities are somewhat akin to those of a nursery school anywhere, except that the children are less likely to make rapid advances in learning and that many of them are likely to remain nursery material for most of their lives.

Nursery, junior, and senior sections may carry out their activities either indoors, outdoors or both according to the time of year and ready access to outdoor play areas direct or almost direct from classrooms is needed.

Storage is required in conjunction with each section or classroom and this storage should be larger in area and capacity than that attached to classrooms in ordinary schools.

9. BELVUE SCHOOL (EDUCATIONALLY SUBNORMAL CHILDREN) NORTHOLT, EALING.
Interior view of a nursery classroom.
Architect: The Austin-Smith Salmon Lord Partnership in Association with T. I'Anson, A.R.I.B.A., Borough Architect, London Borough of Ealing.

Activities within the main sections are likely to include all or some of the following:

Nursery Group

Play activities—ages 3-8 approx.

See-saw.
Rocking horse.
Play pens.
Large wooden blocks.
Toys of many sorts: usual nursery
    toys plus a large variety of domestic objects.
Musical instruments.
Wendy house and similar play structures.

Juniors—ages 8-12 approx.

Many of the Nursery Group objects and play activities. Large nursery toys are no longer used however and there is an element of learning and educational discipline. Painting and similar activities are used. Physical education is introduced.

Seniors

Girls   Sewing
           Cooking
           Washing
           Make-up and personal appearance—dress sense.

Boys   Woodwork
           Gardening

Both   Animals (pets)
           Painting
           Musical instruments (not necessarily
               used very skilfully, but often with a
               marked sense of rhythm).
           Ball games and P.E.

It will thus be seen that practical pursuits play a very large part in senior activities and for this reason "practical" rooms should be provided. The planning brief for such rooms is considered at a later stage together with an investigation of the detail planning.

Special Care Units have not so far been considered. These are sometimes built as an entirely separate building, possibly even on a different site, or as a part of a large group forming a Junior Training Centre. The latter arrangement is probably best in that it provides a more flexible framework and enables children to be placed more readily on an experimental basis. No-one has yet clearly defined the functions of a Special Care Unit except as a section for those children who cannot readily be placed in one of the other sections because of special problems or difficulties. Thus, the sort of children who will find themselves in the Special Care Unit are those, for instance, who have particular emotional or behaviour problems, those who are so completely withdrawn as to be incapable of participating in any group activity and those who have physical disabilities in addition to other problems.

Returning to the subject of activities, it will thus be appreciated that three or four groups will be formed and occupied in their own ways at the start of the morning.

Breaks

There is a break at 11 a.m. when the children have milk but there is no clearly defined break between "work" and "play" as in the normal school. The staff arrange their individual mid-morning break according to the local situation, since constant supervision is required. The average staff break is of ten minutes duration and staff adjourn, no doubt thankfully, to a staff room for this purpose.

Meals

The midday meal is taken by the children in a dining room or hall, usually a large room which may serve both this and a multiplicity of other general purposes, though separate dining accommodation is preferable and is favoured by supervisors.

Numbers in the school are relatively small and the hall is thus not as large as a normal school hall, but serves somewhat similar purposes. It is used for group rhythmic occupations, dancing and simple gymnastics; it normally holds the school piano and is used for music making and may also be used for team games as well as for "shows" and for parent/teacher meetings and other similar evening activities. Storage for chairs and tables is required and these are set out for dining at midday, often by the children, under guidance. A separate dining hall is desirable but may be ruled out on the grounds of cost relative to hours of use.

Depending on local arrangements the kitchen may be for full and complete preparation of meals or, alternatively, it may be only a kitchen for re-heating or final preparation of meals delivered to the school. In either case however, good storage facilities are needed, as well as wash-up arrangements, an area for refuse bins and other usual requirements of kitchen planning.

The kitchens are run by kitchen staff who are recruited and operate quite independently from the teaching and supervisory staff. Sometimes one or two of the older children are able to assist in the kitchen, and this is in line with the policy of helping them to become independent and to fit usefully into jobs in society wherever possible.

The midday meal is sometimes collected by the children on a self-service basis and only the smallest and the most difficult are served, though of course good

10. RESIDENTIAL HOSTEL, BLETCHLEY, BUCKS.
Dining Room showing type of table setting and service counter with kitchen beyond.
F. B. Pooley, F.R.I.B.A., A.M.T.P.I., F.R.I.C.S., County Architect, Buckinghamshire
County Council.

1703475

supervision and periodic assistance are needed. A more common arrangement is for meals to be laid out on plates by the serving "staff" and for some of the children to act as prefects and serve the rest. This helps to produce a sense of usefulness and responsibility and is nearer to a domestic and home situation.

On the whole the children eat well and untoward incidents are not very common. The midday break usually lasts one hour.

After the meal, nursery groups and young children rest on portable camp beds for a short time.

Afternoon activities are very similar to those of the morning. Younger children receive more frequent toilet reminders, though at all ages reminders are necessary for at least some of the children.

Incontinence is a problem with a certain number and in some cases bathing and a change of clothes is necessary.

The afternoon ends between 3 p.m. and 4 p.m. and the children change their shoes, collect their coats and are ushered onto the coach for the return journey.

Activities—residential hostels

The central place of activity for younger children is the Junior Training School, but numerous other types of building are needed if the problem of mental handicap is to be considered in its totality. Most children attend centres

As far as possible living should be subdivided into small
'house groups' with staff 'house parents'

Some activities, such as pet keeping and gardening might
centre on the house

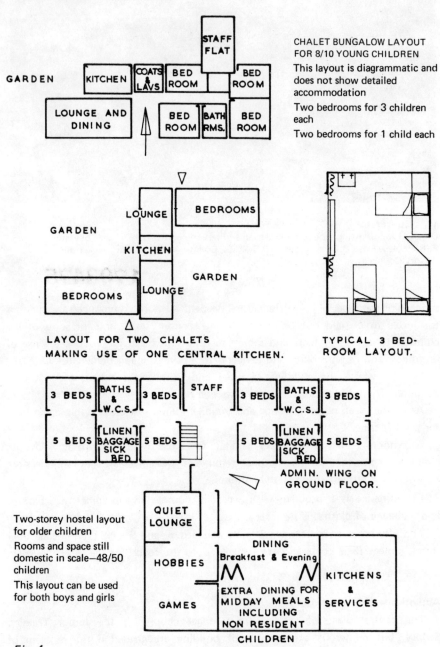

CHALET BUNGALOW LAYOUT
FOR 8/10 YOUNG CHILDREN

This layout is diagrammatic and
does not show detailed
accommodation

Two bedrooms for 3 children
each

Two bedrooms for 1 child each

LAYOUT FOR TWO CHALETS
MAKING USE OF ONE CENTRAL KITCHEN.

TYPICAL 3 BED-
ROOM LAYOUT.

ADMIN. WING ON
GROUND FLOOR.

Two-storey hostel layout
for older children

Rooms and space still
domestic in scale—48/50
children

This layout can be used
for both boys and girls

Fig. 4

36

on a day basis but there is a minority who either have no home, or whose home is unsuitable.

As the children grow older (and larger) some of them also prove "unsuitable" for a normal home background, either through behaviour problems or simply because their parents can no longer cope with them. Extreme cases will probably go to a hospital, but hostels provide an intermediary stage and form a background to which some children appear to respond.

Activity is a relatively straightforward and obvious matter as far as the use of these buildings is concerned, since the chief purpose of such a building is to provide "home" conditions for the hours when the children are not at the school or centre.

The buildings may have a direct link with the centre by means of a covered way or something similar, or may be at a slight distance.

The children sleep in dormitories or small bedrooms according to need and likely response, the numbers to a room thus varying between one and six. They are mostly able to wash and dress themselves, but need staff supervision and assistance to varying degrees. Constant supervision of a hospital type is not needed.

Breakfast is at about 8 a.m. leaving ample time for tidying up and a start to the normal activities of the "school" day or working day at nine o'clock.

The daytime routine is similar for both resident and non-resident children at the centre, unit or workshop.

At 4 p.m. the resident children go back to their own hostel, where they are received and follow the routine they might expect if they were in their own home, namely the hanging up of coats, etc., followed by play activities with tea at 4.30-5.0 p.m.

Play after tea is followed by the gradual withdrawal and preparation for bed of the younger children, the whole process lasting to about 7.30 p.m.

At weekends some children return to their own homes, the others follow a normal domestic routine as far as possible under the guidance of the warden or matron and helpers.

Children at a residential hostel will probably vary widely in attainment though they would not be allocated a place unless they had been assessed as suitable.

Some are remarkably capable and may be employed in workshops at the unit or nearby or may even have started going out to work. Some may live at the hostel during the week and return home at weekends. Often in these cases they are almost capable or entering normal life but lack the final confidence or need the overall care and supervision which hostel routine and a qualified supervisor can give.

Activities—special units

The children nearly all attend on a day basis, arriving by coach and keeping school hours as for the Junior Training School children.

Activities are similar to those of the nursery group in the Junior Training

37

SPECIAL CARE

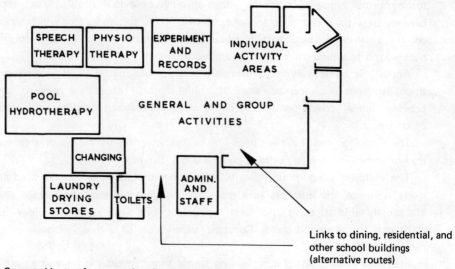

Suggested layout for comprehensive special care facilities
Diagram illustrating main spaces and their relationship

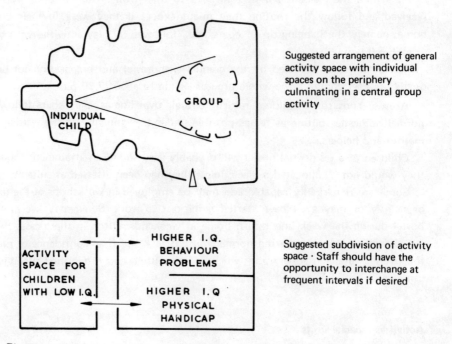

Suggested arrangement of general activity space with individual spaces on the periphery culminating in a central group activity

Suggested subdivision of activity space · Staff should have the opportunity to interchange at frequent intervals if desired

Fig. 5

38

School but are likely to be even more informal, spasmodic and "play-orientated" and, whereas children in the other groups have the ability to play and learn as a group or series of groups to some extent, those in the Special Unit are likely to carry on their activities as a series of individuals. Many of these activities may appear either messy or destructive or both to the normal by-stander, but the designer should remember that this will probably not be a view shared by the teachers and psychiatrists concerned.

Sand play and water play are both popular with many of the children. Normal nursery toys such as see-saws and rocking horses are used. Play pens may be used as well as large building blocks, planks, large toys of many varieties and a large and often bizarre assortment of objects which may even include such things as old telephones, hammers and nails, and surplus wireless sets.

Some activities using this equipment will thus be very noisy, especially as they are usually enjoyed on a repetitive and obsessive basis. At the same time other children may wish for quiet and possibly even for solitude and will withdraw as far as possible.

The objective of supervisors and workers is to try to interest the children in objects and surroundings, to try to communicate with them, to coax them into learning and wishing to learn and to further their development both social and mental to a stage at which they would be able to move to the appropriate level in the Junior Training School.

Apart from these general observations about activities the designer should bear in mind one or two points which may easily not be realised. One is that most of the children do not talk — not necessarily because they lack the physical equipment but because for one reason or another they have never learned.

The second is that they operate as single individuals and are very liable to sudden and inexplicable changes of mood and feeling.

The third is that they are particularly liable to unclean behaviour and must be encouraged to improve their habits. The provision of facilities assisting the staff in dealing with these points is especially important.

The fourth is that there may well be cot cases or chair cases in the Special Unit, and children with physical as well as mental disabilities will pose numerous problems in terms of planning and environment.

Work/therapy—sheltered workshops

The role of sheltered workshops belongs to the Adult Training Centre but is listed here and described briefly since some of the older children find a place in these workshops. Their main purpose is to provide occupations for older children and adults in which they can be persuaded to take an interest, in which they can develop their thinking and relate this to developing a skill or skills, and in which as a result they often develop a certain pride and self-sufficiency. In a sense it often provides a form of therapy and also something which shows them a way to earning a small amount of money. This helps in the process of developing self-help and self-reliance.

The workshops are usually adjacent to a larger group of buildings which may include an adult centre, a junior centre and possibly a residential hostel, or they may be part of a hospital complex.

They are not planned or equipped to carry out any very precise or specific work but are designed to give facilities for carrying out a wide variety of possible

11 and 12. SHELTERED WORKSHOP, BLETCHLEY, BUCKS.
Typical layout and type of equipment used. The interior is well lit and particularly pleasant.
Lower picture shows heavier machine section.
F. B. Pooley, F.R.I.B.A., A.M.T.P.I., F.R.I.C.S., County Architect, Buckinghamshire
County Council.

activities, nearly all of them involving manual work. Woodworking and metalworking of a simple type are usually carried on, together with assembly work varying from the connection or assembly of two or three very small components up to the making of large boxes, wardrobes, cupboards, and similar items.

A certain amount of raw materials and components awaiting assembly are usually kept in store, as well as a quantity of assembled or finished goods awaiting despatch.

Some children prove themselves interested in the workshops quite early, especially if they have grown and developed quickly. Some find a definite therapeutic value and will vary their "job" according to their dominant mood of the day. There are occasions when a disturbed boy will work off his feelings through the operation of a press or a wire bending machine in a very satisfactory manner! Surprisingly there is very seldom a case of either injury or damage.

Recreation—out-of-doors

Within the centre there are usually large outdoor play areas. Play is far more common than formal learning, though often used to stimulate interest and to teach indirectly.

Access is usually direct from the indoor rooms including the indoor dining space or hall.

Organised games are sometimes possible with the older children but generally only at the senior level. Sheltered outdoor play space is also provided but whilst shelter from cold winds is desirable shelter from rain might just as easily be achieved by returning to the classrooms since access is direct and simple.

Areas of grass are employed as well as paved or tarmac areas. Landscaping to give interest is an important matter. This should not be too sophisticated but there is no doubt that some "softening" of the landscape plays an important visual role.

Open play space

The proportion of open play space should be larger than that provided in normal schools. The children are unlikely to be able to spend much time on formal academic work but often enjoy doing things with their hands and learning movement and co-ordination so that, in addition to normal play facilities, many other outdoor features are worth consideration, such as adventure play features, climbing frames, swings and see-saws. Care and imagination are needed in the design and layout to ensure that the children gain the maximum benefit and make the widest possible use of the material, but with minimum hazard. For example, swings should be isolated from ball games and from walking children to avoid accidents. Likewise, climbing frames and adventure features such as tree trunks should be on soft ground so that injury from falls is minimised.

It is vital that the children should be stimulated and encouraged to look

D

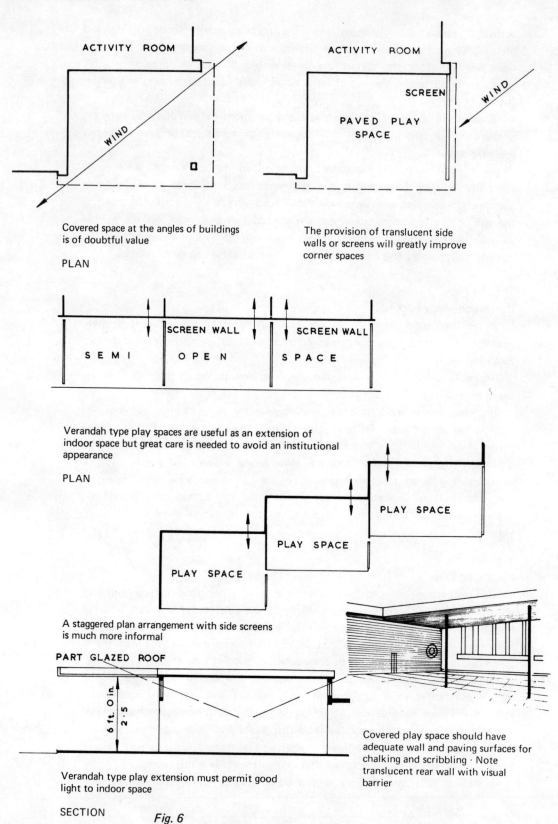

ACTIVITY ROOM

WIND

Covered space at the angles of buildings
is of doubtful value

PLAN

ACTIVITY ROOM

SCREEN

PAVED PLAY
SPACE

WIND

The provision of translucent side
walls or screens will greatly improve
corner spaces

SEMI   OPEN   SPACE
SCREEN WALL   SCREEN WALL

Verandah type play spaces are useful as an extension of
indoor space but great care is needed to avoid an institutional
appearance

PLAN

PLAY SPACE

PLAY SPACE

PLAY SPACE

A staggered plan arrangement with side screens
is much more informal

PART GLAZED ROOF

6 ft. 0 in.
2·5

Verandah type play extension must permit good
light to indoor space

Covered play space should have
adequate wall and paving surfaces for
chalking and scribbling · Note
translucent rear wall with visual
barrier

SECTION   *Fig. 6*

42

outward, to use the facilities provided and to prove to themselves that they can acquit themselves well both physically and mentally. At the same time, they must be safeguarded as much as possible from dangers, not only because of physical hurt but because of the mental discouragement which would inevitably follow. To design features which will combine these qualities and safeguards, the architect must be subtle, imaginative, sympathetic and human! Above all, he must be a realist.

Many cases exist where internal courtyards have been planned with shrubs and trees which either will not grow or have never even been planted. Courtyards exist in Junior Training Schools which have been planned with small ornamental pools which are quite useless and unsuitable. The architect must face the fact that he is spending public money and this must be employed to stimulate and help both children and staff. There is no scope for "penthouse" techniques and there is no scope for designing with the professional magazines in mind. Every detail must be of practical help. It is sobering to find that wherever internal courtyards have been created, the usual comment is that they would make good sheltered play areas. This is a comment worth exploring

Sheltered play

Sheltered play areas are highly desirable and are insufficiently provided. Generally speaking, a sheltered play are should have not only a protective roof covering, but also walls providing shelter from cold winds. Ideally, it would take the form either of a semi-covered "verandah" type of structure, or of a deeper paved play area with a translucent roof and with walls on two or even on three sides protecting it from prevailing winds.

Weather conditions can be very trying and troublesome for some of the mentally handicapped. For example, mongol children are particularly prone to chest complaints and therefore, affected by cold winds and draughts. Likewise, many of the children sun-burn easily and are adversely affected by over strong sunlight.

Sheltered play areas must be truly sheltered and must not be just roofed-in wind tunnels. Wall areas are also useful in providing not only shelter but also the necessary background for many kinds of ball games which stimulate and help in teaching co-ordination and fostering skill and independence.

Pools

Both outdoor and indoor pools allow for "dabbling" and water play and for actual swimming. Many love water and it is considered to have a therapeutic value for some of the disturbed children. Attempts at swimming lead to better co-ordination of limbs. Indoor pools are more easily supervised and controlled and are more readily capable of use throughout the year.

13. OPEN AIR PLAY AREA SERVING DAY ACTIVITY ROOMS, SHREWSBURY.
Architect: G. W. Hamlyn Dip.Arch.A.R.I.B.A., County Architect, Salop County Council.
Formerly Ralph Crowe, A.A.Dip.A.R.I.B.A.)

14 and 15. PADDLING POOL AND OPEN AIR PLAY SPACE SERVING NURSERY UNIT, GLOUCESTER.
John R. Sketchley, A.R.I.B.A., Dip.T.P.A.M.T.P.I., City Architect. (Formerly J. V. Wall, A.R.I.B.A.)

44

15.

Activities—detail planning

Many activities carried on in the various buildings already considered are common to all or most of them. Detail planning is therefore investigated under the heading of each activity in turn rather than under the heading of a specific building type.

Arrival—reception—classrooms

The length of the approach will obviously depend on the shape and size of the individual site, so that at some city buildings, coaches will virtually pull in off the road whilst in many other cases there may be quite a long drive from the site boundary.

It is preferable to adopt a "drive" type of approach as far as possible. Any building involving a number of people requires good car parking facilities but apart from the necessary width for passing and turning vehicles it is better to keep parking near the main entrance reasonably unobtrusive. In this way it will be possible to provide for an approach to the entrance which is reasonably small and personal in scale. The planting of shrubs, grass, and the adoption of an informal curb line will all help to achieve this and the aim should be to avoid anything in the nature of an "institutional" type of appearance.

Even in recently built centres there are numerous cases where on arrival the coaches swing through large iron gates and drive over a "sea" of tarmac straight up to large double doors, giving the impression that yet another intake has arrived at the barracks rather than that thirty or so disturbed children have arrive for another day of play and "teaching".

The scale of the design should be as human and sympathetic to the children as possible and the feeling reasonably homelike in character. This is not to say that the building should imitate a house. A building which accommodates eighty or more children and staff is clearly not a house and in some respects handicapped children are remarkably clear-sighted. At the same time the scale and feeling of normal home surroundings are worth preserving and adopting as far as possible.

Entrance

The entrance itself presents a design problem. Conventional double doors will automatically enlarge the scale. Many existing centres have wide imposing double doors of bank-like appearance which are seldom both used and which are in any case quite unnecessary. The largest number of people likely to use the doors at any one time will be about thirty, and this will only occur at a few specific times early in the day and on going home again.

The largest object needing access through the doors will be a wheel chair, the minimum width being 840 mm (2 ft 9 in) and this also is not a very frequent occurrence. For the rest of the day the doors will not be used at all except by occasional chance callers.

From this it may be deduced that a fairly wide single door would be perfectly adequate, giving a clear width of 900 mm (3 ft).

On disembarking from the bus the children should be able to approach the door under cover provided by a canopy. The entrance itself should be well sited to afford shelter from prevailing winds and driving rain, and protection provided by recessing the door, by a projecting angle of the building or by wing walls, is very useful for this purpose.

Draught lobbies are not usually provided, since they are not merely un-homelike in appearance but cause considerable complications in shepherding the children.

If steps are needed to the entrance these should be very broad and shallow and a shallow ramp may be preferable for wheel chairs.

Doors should open inward and should not be double action swing doors if this is avoidable. Fire-escape requirements may affect this but since the buildings are usually planned on a generous horizontal basis it should be possible to achieve fire-escape by other means.

Entrance doors are usually fully glazed, providing the maximum light and visibility, making them as safe as possible in use, and the glazing should be clear

16. ENTRANCE HALL OF RESIDENTIAL HOSTEL, BLETCHLEY, BUCKS.
The building is used only by older children who are able to take an increasingly responsible attitude to everyday life.
F. B. Pooley, F.R.I.B.A., A.M.T.P.I., F.R.I.C.S., County Architect, Buckinghamshire County Council.

and wired. Push-plates and furniture should be set fairly low. If plates are selected, a vertical design can be used to cater for people of various heights. Although the children will not be using the main entrance door except at arrival and departure, some of them like to "help" and take the initiative in simple things like opening doors. The accomplishment of this sort of operation often gives them considerable satisfaction and helps breed confidence, and doors should not therefore be too heavy or have door furniture of a type or in a position which could not be operated by a nine- or ten-year-old.

To obtain greater light at the entrance, windows or side lights may be used. Top light should be used discreetly and not unless there is no practicable alternative.

Hall/Foyer

The first impression on entering is of great importance. Whether the child is arriving at the centre for the first time or not, his first view inside the building must create a definite impression. This can be played down to a domestic scale, suggesting small domestic activities such as hanging up a coat, or it might be used to attract the child's attention and interest in a particular way, and this is a matter which must be left for consultation between the designer, the medical

47

authority and educationalists. The important point, however, is that there is not only scope but an active requirement for conscious planning and design.

Things seen should not be the accidental result of casual and careless planning. In particular there should not be a view straight down a long corridor, since this is particularly impersonal and institutional and lacking in positive directional help to the child. Direction can often be contrived as an element of both the planning and the design if careful thought is given.

Coat areas

The children's first act on entering the building should be to hang up their coats and to remove their outdoor shoes and put on their slippers or light shoes. Coat hanging areas should thus be close to the entrance and if possible to their own classrooms.

Nursery problems are slightly different and are dealt with elsewhere.

Numbers are far smaller than in ordinary schools and the junior and senior sections are unlikely to have more than about fifteen boys and fifteen girls in each, making a total of sixty to eighty children in all (excluding nursery section).

Coat-hanging space is thus a smaller and more informal part of the plan than in other educational buildings. Hanging up of coats and changing of shoes is a simple social activity which the children are encouraged to acquire. Juniors and seniors may use the same areas if numbers are small, or may have small sub areas adjoining their classrooms. Pegs are placed at two heights say 760 mm (30 in) and 1 050 mm (42 in) to allow for variation in size and capabilities. A bench or seat about 350 mm (14 in) high is usually placed under the pegs with a shelf or shoe rail under it. This is a better arrangement than positioning the seat elsewhere, as coat and shoes are readily identifiable together.

There are several variations possible in planning. For example, in some buildings, coats and shoes are changed on a moveable bench/hanging fitting which is then wheeled into a cupboard. In nursery units coats are often hung within the entrance to the room itself.

The children usually have their own specific peg and shoe space, and are encouraged always to use the same one. Their own name is often printed on a coloured slip and placed beside the peg to help them recognise their own written name and associate it with their own personal belongings. Other types of sign and symbol are sometimes used, and the provision of an inset panel suitable for writing or attaching signs and words might be considered. Mounting height would not be more than 1 050 mm (42 in) and probably level with the pegs.

The process of removing coats and changing shoes is carried out under general staff supervision. The head or supervisor's room is placed near the main entrance, enabling him or her to note arrivals and departures, supervise the start and completion of the day and attend to daytime callers. Observation is desirable from the supervisors room both of the entrance hall and the approach from outside.

From the coat space the children will move on to the toilets before entering their own "classrooms", another small but necessary piece of social training.

17. BELVUE SCHOOL (EDUCATIONALLY SUBNORMAL CHILDREN),
NORTHOLT, EALING.
Coat space formed by widening the circulation near classrooms.
Architect: The Austin-Smith Salmon Lord Partnership in Association with T. I'Anson,
Borough Architect, London Borough of Ealing.

Toilets

Toilets training can easily become something of a fetish in dealing with small children and this is especially true for mentally handicapped children who are often casual about personal cleanliness and even downright uncooperative in some cases, so that an unusual stress may be laid on efforts to put the situation right.

In nursery rooms the toilets are sometimes entered directly off the classroom. Wash-basins are in the room itself, usually with some simple form of space division, such as a low cupboard fitting and possibly a change in flooring colour or material to suggest the different purpose. Children have individual personal towels. Size of basin and mounting height are important and are varied according to whether the room is nursery, junior or senior. In the latter two cases mirrors are desirable and again the mounting height must be suited to age and size. Plumbing is dealt with in more detail in a later chapter.

Divisions between W.C. compartments are lower and simpler than in adult installations and give the children privacy from one another but assist staff supervision.

Sluice and laundry

A bath or shower and a sluice room are provided close to the toilets for dealing with pots for very young children and for dirty clothing. Detailed layout of services is considered in the chapter on Services. Laundry facilities may vary from a simple washer and spin dryer in the case of a small day unit, to quite elaborate and heavy laundry installations in the case of a residential hostel. It is very common experience that the usual sluice and laundry provisions are inadequate for needs, especially bearing in mind that all facilities are normally run to one hundred per cent capacity.

In the case of residential hostels, laundry facilities are frequently shared with other buildings, such as a day centre, forming a larger group of buildings. Toilet and bath arrangements within a hostel are mostly of a normal pattern, similar to those in an ordinary house, except that a greater number of fittings are provided. The bathrooms and W.C.s are arranged so that each small group of from four to twelve children has its own facilities, rather than having one large central installation.

Classrooms

During the normal school week "learning" activities centre largely on the classrooms, though the term "classrooms" must be interpreted liberally. In a broad sense the children are learning every minute of the day, but formal educational discipline does not feature largely in this.

In the nursery classes up to about the age of eight, the children spend most of their time in play. Large nursery toys often have an educational value and during these years the children are learning to co-ordinate their movements better, to talk and communicate wherever possible, to co-operate in group activities, to identify by shape, by pattern and colour, and many other activities up to the limit of their abilities.

Rooms for this purpose are of average classroom size or slightly larger say 40-60 m^2 (400-650 ft^2). They are rather crowded with equipment, and very full and ample storage is needed. No desks are used and the usual appearance is that of a light, cheerful but inevitably crowded nursery. Ceilings should not be high—2.5-3 m (8-9 ft). Low window cills giving a view outside are not absolutely necessary but it is an advantage if the room communicates directly with outside play areas. The design of fittings is important and these are considered in a later chapter.

Children like to explore and this outward looking trend can be stimulated either by planning rooms which are not uncompromisingly rectangular (for example L-shaped or polygonal), or by dividing the room shape by means of moveable and flexibly planned fittings. Flexibility in planning is a very important matter and some medical officers have expressed the view that what is needed is quite simply space, with the maximum possibilities to vary and sub-divide.

In many cases nursery sections are divided into two classes, beginners and a sort of unofficial upper level, beyond which there are possibly two junior

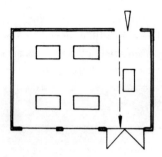

Typical layout plan of activity
space for up to 20
children as provided in
existing day centres

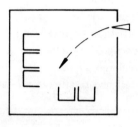

Use of individual
'activity booths'
may attract the child
Square plan shape is
too finite and emphatic

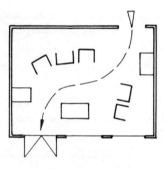

Layout plan improved by using
a mixture of 'activity booths'
and tables and a more interesting
circulation route making full use
of the room

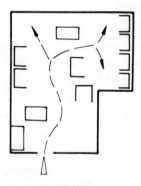

Modification of plan
shape to increase the
interest and provide for
different areas of activity

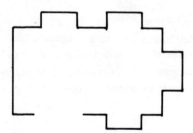

Rectangular room plan varied to provide
a larger number of 'private corners' and
spaces for individual activity

Department of education and science
building bulletin No. 27 shows further
useful layouts

Fig. 7

Provision of individual activity
spaces in a less finite manner
may encourage mixing and
sociability
Use of walls curved on plan may
help in this

sections. The first nursery class often rests at midday on small camp beds for which storage is required. The average size of class depends on the total number of children but is between ten and twenty.

Junior classrooms are similar to the nursery classrooms but there is an increasing element of educational discipline. There is still unlikely to be any provision of desks and the room is not usually orientated towards a focal point occupied by a teacher. Instead, teaching takes place in small groups in which the children sit round informally. Much of it is semi-social as well as informative and designed to stimulate interest and develop thought.

Practical rooms

Senior classes have a marked increase in the orderliness of the room and a feeling of tidiness and organisation. Again the level of teaching has been raised though it is still semi-social. There is generally a strong interest in practical work and for the senior children a practical room should be provided, or perhaps a "practical" section extended from the normal classroom area.

The room may be used for weaving, woodwork, assembly of articles, and all kinds of similar practical work in which many of the children take great interest and derive real satisfaction.

The girls also learn cooking, sewing, washing and ironing, and similar domestic practical work as well as make-up and the rudiments of shopping.

The layout of a practical room thus requires very careful planning. All classrooms need a separate store room but storage for practical rooms should be correspondingly larger, say 6.50-7.50 m^2 (70-80 ft^2).

Unless there is a separate kitchen for domestic training the practical room should be planned in such a way that a small but realistic kitchen set-up can be provided similar to a normal house kitchen. This need not be fully enclosed but may be on two or three walls, perhaps partly achieved by a spatial sub-division within the practical room.

If numbers require it, the provision of at least two cookers and similar duplication of other fittings may be necessary.

Woodwork needs a similar subsection with the provision of two or three work benches, tool storage and a proper store for timber and similar materials.

Toilets for the senior classrooms are no longer virtually within the room but should be reached without undue travel distance or complication. Boys and girls toilets are separate but the classes themselves are, of course, mixed.

Dining space

A dining-room is an essential part of the buildings whether for day care or residential use. In order to achieve economies in building cost the function of eating is sometimes combined with other uses by dining in a school hall or in a lounge. This arrangement is not popular with most of those in charge of such

EFFECT OF PLAN SHAPE

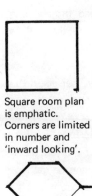

Square room plan
is emphatic.
Corners are limited
in number and
'inward looking'.

Screens or fittings
used to increase
variety.

Polygonal plan shape gives
more 'corners for individual
retreat', but corners with
obtuse angles which are
'outward looking'.

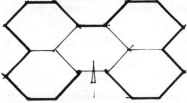

Grouped polygonal plan form gives
varied 'activity areas' with good
lines for supervision.

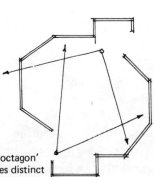

'Broken octagon'
form gives distinct
activity areas and
good lines for
supervision.

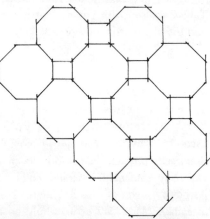

Grouped polygons capable of sub-division to
form several rooms or activity areas.
Care is needed to avoid 'forced' or stylised
planning.

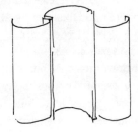
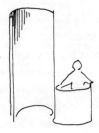

Use of combinations of free-standing 'booths' to form corners or islands for
individual activities.

Fig. 8

buildings and it is preferable to have a separate dining-room. The use of a school hall for this purpose results in considerable interruption of other activities, the constant setting out and removal of chairs and tables, the necessity for a large storage area for the chairs and tables, and of course the need for cleaning and the removal of food scraps and crumbs after every meal before the hall can be used again.

In a residental building a dining area could be an off-shoot of a lounge, perhaps even with a suitable folding partition or space divider, but again the two functions should be clearly separate.

Where a day centre and hostel are combined, the dining-room is essential and is often a point of linkage between the two buildings, a place in which boarders have breakfast and the teatime meal and all children have their midday meal.

It is desirable to provide a separate route by which access can be gained from the hostel to the day centre without passing through the dining-room.

In combined buildings a kitchen is essential as food is prepared and cooked on the premises. Dry goods store, cold storage, service entrance, bin and refuse store, and kitchen staff toilets are all required.

Ordinary crockery and cutlery is usual and there are very few breakages. Tables are set with cutlery but meals are fully set out on plates at the servery and there is no tureen service.

The hall and its functions

In day centres a hall is provided as a sort of large general purpose space. It is used for rhythm and movement classes, dancing, attempts at mime and dramatics, physical education—which requires the setting up of equipment and which is valuable in aiding co-ordination—and for a wide variety of other purposes such as team games, teacher/parent meetings, school plays and assembly. Many day centres hold an assembly, some as the first activity of the day and some as the last. It is short and though it may be questioned whether the children really understand much about it, at least it gives some sort of corporate feeling—perhaps a feeling of belonging.

Since the hall is used for this variety of functions it is essentially a larger space, the size depending on the number of children but likely to be 90-140 m^2 (1 000-1 600 ft^2) in area. Height is 3.6-4.25 m (12-14 ft) and is partly governed by the use of equipment for physical education and ball games.

Storage is needed for equipment. A conventional stage is not required but some form of portable sectional platform is very useful. The possibility of using plan shapes other than the rectangle has been investigated at various times and there may be scope for devising a hall which has space extending from it in various ways and at various heights. The hall has important functions and should not be a central circulation space giving sole access to various other rooms. This is, unfortunately, often the case and causes interruption and distraction.

ASSEMBLY HALLS

A main activity space used for large groups · Also for smaller groups needing a large indoor
space · Used for: Music and movement
Adventure apparatus
Rhythm and dancing
Gymnastics
Simple dramatics · Self-expression
Ball games · Team games
Parent/teacher functions
Group film displays

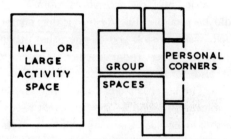

RELATIONSHIP OF HALL TO OTHER ACTIVITY SPACES

The hall should be capable of use without interruption · It should be
capable of subdivision to obtain maximum use, but should not be used
as a circulation route

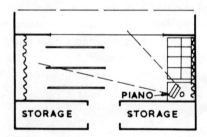

Raised platform built up of mobile
box sections
A formal stage is not needed
Piano has maximum control position
Soft hangings are useful to give
domestic scale and atmosphere
Storage needed for large and heavy
equipment

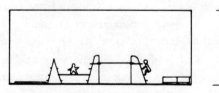

Typical layout for indoor adventure
course

Section through hall showing artificial
lighting

Avoid the use of
breakable or open-type
lighting fittings

Fig. 9

Staff needs—day centres

Reference has already been made to the supervisor's room — equivalent of the headmaster's study and a room which should be near the main entrance and have a view of the entrance area. In this room the supervisor or head receives visitors, interviews staff and conducts day-to-day administrative business. It should be light, airy, cheerful, of reasonable size (say about 12-14 m^2 (120-150 ft^2)) and conducive to work, much of which requires careful thought.

If it is not possible to have a second small room for conducting interviews then a distinct waiting area should be provided near the supervisors room.

A medical examination room should be provided for use by visiting doctors. This will contain an examination couch, scales, a sink and all the usual fittings. As an alternative, some centres have a larger room used not only for examinations by visiting doctors but also for regular day to day work by a physiotherapist and/or a speech therapist. The latter is a great asset since physical capacity—especially speech and communication—is one of the first great needs if the child is to develop. Such a room should be near the main entrance. A staff room is needed and this should be quiet, restful and insulated from noise and from un-announced "visitors". There is a considerable strain on staff working with mentally handicapped children, and although they have very little free time in which to make use of the staff room, they should have every possible facility for calm and rest when the opportunity presents itself. The main requirements are a pleasant, restful atmosphere, facilities for quiet thought and writing and for discussion with other members of the staff. Sometimes the staff's own midday meal is taken in the staff room after helping with the children.

Staff toilets are required—usually one W.C. and washing facilities for male staff and similar facilities for female staff, who are probably more numerous.

Observation and recording

Treatment and cure are medical and psychological problems, many aspects of which still require a great deal of research before a solution is likely to be found.

Such research can only be carried out against a background of enquiry and investigation and a careful recording and evaluating of facts. At the present time little observation or fact-recording appears to take place on any systematic basis and there is certainly no national or international exchange of such information other than through the medium of articles and papers in professional publications and at conferences.

Most of the observation work currently carried out is on a purely voluntary and self-starting basis, by such staff as may be interested, and conclusions and action, if any, are personal and intuitive. The work depends almost entirely on the quality of the staff and on the amount of time they can spare for this aspect of their work. The architect can help to some extent by affording facilities for observation which are as easy to use and as far ranging as possible.

In existing buildings the question of observation does not seem to have been given the importance it merits. Fixed glass panels are sometimes provided in the

PURPOSES   General supervision and control (staff)
Investigation of
behaviour and needs   (staff and specialists)
Research

METHODS   Direct observation by staff and helpers
Indirect observation by specialists
Visual observation is greatly improved if
audio aids are available in specialist/staff
rooms
Children often refuse to behave naturally
and are unsettled under open observation
by visitors
Central position required within activity
spaces

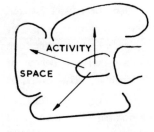

Glass observation panels should be
curtained and resemble ordinary
windows

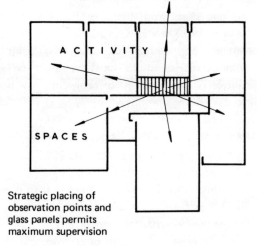

Strategic placing of
observation points and
glass panels permits
maximum supervision

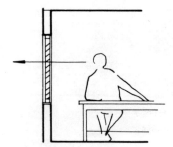

Specialist and staff
observation from
special point (staff or
research room) · Low
cill with blinds for
partial concealment

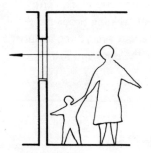
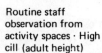

Routine staff
observation from
activity spaces · High
cill (adult height)

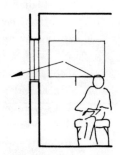

Specialist and staff
observation · High cill
for concealment and
use of angled mirror

Fig. 10

E

form of a single fixed light in walls between corridor and "classroom". Sometimes there may also be single fixed lights between classrooms and the supervisor's room, between one classroom and another, or between the supervisor's room and play spaces or dining-room, but the arrangements are often haphazard and unsystematic.

In almost all cases single fixed lights are provided, formed of clear or wired plate glass, the size varying from about 600 x 600 mm (2 x 2 ft) to 1.8 x 0.9 m (6 x 3 ft). Cill height is usually between 0.9 and 1.2 m (3 and 4 ft).

Panels or lights may be set in line to enable the supervisor to see through several rooms or in several directions, but this "central room" type of arrangement is more likely to be encountered in units attached to hospitals than in ordinary day centres. On the whole it is true to say that the degree of "central vision" and observation is no greater in the ordinary day centre or hostel than in the average ordinary school.

If one starts from the basic premise that more methodical observation and proper record keeping would be an asset to experts considering the question of treatment and perhaps of care, then facilities within the building are vital. Certain basic questions must therefore be posed and answered before the architect is in a position to incorporate the necessary facilities and performance into any building proposals.

These basic questions are as follows:
1. Who or what is to be observed?
   The children at the centre
      —their total behaviour from arrival to departure.
      —their reactions to specific situations.
      —their behaviour to one another.
      —the effect upon them of environment.
      —their use of objects and equipment.
      —their method of tackling problems.
   (In summary, just about everything about them.)
2. Who will carry out the observations?
   Permanent staff
   Social workers
   Class workers
   Supervisors
   Resident specialists—if any
   Visiting specialists
3. When will observations be carried out?
   The possibility should exist at all times even though it may not necessarily always be utilised.
4. How will observations be carried out?
   Direct observation by helpers and social workers who are in close contact with the children at the time.

58

Static observation from fixed points or by fixed means incorporated within the building.

5. What form would observation take and how could it be used?

Although observation is a visual matter it requires notes and records and possibly, in some circumstances, photographs to be taken.

In this way a store of recorded data could be built up which would enable search to be made for patterns of behaviour and which would facilitate the comparing of notes and cases with other teachers and other centres. This would probably permit a more scientific evaluation to be made.

It is important that an activity such as observation should be carried out as tactfully and unobtrusively as possible. Children are remarkably sharp and perceptive and this applies as much to certain categories of mentally handicapped child as to any other.

Snooping and obvious deception are not only repugnant in a general sense but will also lead to a breakdown of any confidence which may have been established and possibly to conscious acting by some children.

There are thus two distinct possibilities; namely direct and open observation, which will come to be accepted and therefore forgotten, and observation which is completely concealed.

Open observation from a fixed point is most easily achieved by making use of the supervisor's room — such an arrangement would reasonably permit a measure of observation by visiting experts without arousing any particular notice, since the supervisor deals with all outside visitors.

The average size for a supervisor's room at the present time is about 10-12 m^2 (100-120 ft^2) and this would need to be increased if the room is used regularly for observation and record purposes.

The supervisor (or warden in the case of hostels and workshops) is a very experienced person and even casual observation from this quarter is valuable, but it should be added that he or she is a very busy person concerned with the overall day-to-day running of the building and is unlikely to be in a position to carry out regular work of this nature. It is of considerable importance that the supervisor should be able to see the nature of activity at various points with a minimum of personal movement.

Sight of the main entrance and the space immediately inside it is desirable and also of the approach from outside, if possible. The latter may have to be sacrificed in order to achieve maximum sight lines within the building. It will be apparent that the supervisor's room, though small, is a key point and should command discreet but useful views of as much of the building as is practicable.

Fixed glazing is not only acceptable but probably necessary in order to cut out sound interference. Lights need not be large provided the sight lines are adequate. Consideration should be given as to whether it is preferred to have lights with a fairly high cill level which can only be used when an occupant of the room is standing, and which will therefore give a reasonable privacy when seated at a desk, or whether it may be preferable to have the cills at a fairly low level so that more casual and constant visibility is possible. If the latter course is adopted it should be remembered that privacy within the room will almost certainly be required sometimes and observation windows might therefore be fitted with curtains or venetian blinds. The movement caused by drawing curtains is obtrusive and of the two possibilities, blinds give far greater flexibility in use, permitting casual semi-concealed observation or complete privacy as required, and with less obvious movement during the course of adjustment.

Between one "classroom" and another or between rooms and circulation spaces, panels should have the appearance of normal windows with roughly normal window sizes and cill heights. Although the panels are used only by staff when in a standing position, an unduly high cill level gives an artificial appearance. Such internal panels may be treated as windows in every sense of the word and may be framed by curtains or have wide cills used for plants, toys or other items. The more they are treated as normal windows the more readily acceptable and unobtrusive they are likely to be.

Depending on staffing possibilities and the depth of work which is being undertaken it may be worth considering the provision of an observation and records room as an entirely separate feature, though preferably reached from the supervisor's room — both because of its central position and because of the control which such a position will give. Such a room would be relatively small in area but should have maximum possible sight lines, with especially good visibility to other rooms where a high degree of activity is carried on, such as the main play/classrooms and the practical room.

In terms of space it would be necessary to accommodate several filing cabinets for written and photographic records as well as providing reasonable space for two people.

There are many scientific aids nowadays which might be regarded as desirable but it is doubtful whether some could be used, on grounds of cost. Thus, although it might be valuable to have a photographic record of a particular expression or reaction under particular circumstances, this would obviously call for a well mounted camera with a telephoto lens. It could likewise be agreed that closed-circuit television would give the supervisor, and any qualified expert observers, knowledge of everything which occurred without the need to be seen at all, but again the cost would almost certainly be prohibitive. It is worth considering the use of amplifying equipment, which is relatively inexpensive and which would keep the observer in touch aurally as well as visually.

The central observation and records room would be reached through the supervisor's room for reasons of security and discretion, and could be a very valuable addition in the care of mentally handicapped children.

A logical further development would be the provision of a complete experimental group in which a further space is used as a testing-room in which conditions and equipment can be varied and the results recorded. This, however, would appreciably raise the cost of the building. No such provision has so far been made and although the possibility is examined in more detail in a later chapter it remains purely a personal opinion of the author.

PLAY LEARNING OBSERVATION AND EXPERIMENT—1

PURPOSE OF SPACES To arrange a progression of spaces in which the children would carry out different types of activity · To encourage and stimulate the children to active play and learning · To make a more scientific and systematic observation than has so far been possible and to record the findings

ARRANGEMENT OF SPACES

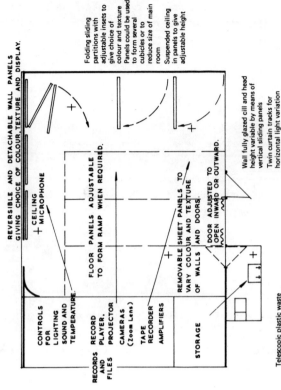

Spaces lead into one another and the child progresses from quiet to more noisy and active pursuits and then to outdoor activities. In alternative plan 2 the procedure can be reversed. Progression is from play to experimental space and back to commencement of play sequence

SUGGESTED PLAN 1.

TOILET
COATS

WATER, SAND AND NOISY PLAY
OBJECT PLAY
QUIET ACTIVITY
OUTDOOR ACTIVITY
EXPERIMENTAL SPACE
OBSERVATION AND RECORDS
OUTDOOR ACTIVITY

SUGGESTED PLAN 2.

TOILET
COATS

WATER SAND AND NOISY PLAY
OBJECT PLAY
QUIET ACTIVITY
OUTDOOR ACTIVITY
OBSERVATION AND RECORDS
EXPERIMENTAL SPACE

NOTE: These layouts are designed for intensive observation and experiment in connection with special care, diagnosis, and allied problems. They reflect the author's own views and are not based on current practice

Fig. 11

PLAY LEARNING OBSERVATION AND EXPERIMENT – 2

EXPERIMENT AND TEST ROOM

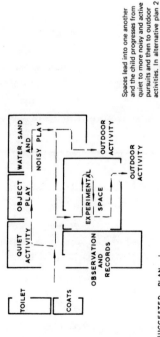
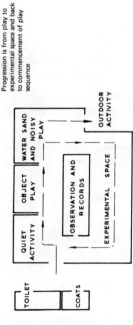

REVERSIBLE AND DETACHABLE WALL PANELS GIVING CHOICE OF COLOUR, TEXTURE AND DISPLAY.

CEILING
MICROPHONE

CONTROLS FOR LIGHTING SOUND AND TEMPERATURE.

FLOOR PANELS ADJUSTABLE TO FORM RAMP WHEN REQUIRED.

RECORD PLAYER, PROJECTOR
CAMERAS (Zoom Lens)
TAPE RECORDER AMPLIFIERS

RECORDS AND FILES

REMOVABLE SHEET PANELS TO VARY COLOUR AND TEXTURE OF WALLS AND DOORS.

DOOR ADJUSTED TO OPEN INWARD OR OUTWARD.

STORAGE

Folding sliding partitions with adjustable insets to give choice of colour and texture Panels could be used to form several cubicles or to reduce size of main room

Suspended ceiling in panels to give adjustable height

Wall fully glazed cill and head height variable by means of vertical sliding panels
Twin curtain tracks for horizontal light variation

Telescopic plastic waste
Height of w.c. and basin variable

PURPOSES
To permit the adjustment of environment and complete but unobtrusive observation and recording by at least two people simultaneously, children may have helper with them in the room or might be alone or in a small group. Direct access from control room is needed

VARIABLES
Floor · Slope or flat plane in sections · Two levels possible within room · Finishes · Ceiling · Height · Slope or flat · Colour · Pattern · Texture · Sound absorption · Room · Size and proportion · Wall finishes · Colour · Pattern and texture · Privacy and character · Smaller rooms or recesses · Furnishing 'mock ups' · Play objects · Preferences ·
Lighting · Extent of windows · Height and position · Toplight ·
Artificial Light · Diffused · Direct · Low/high position ·
Low/high intensity · Coloured lighting ·
Sound · Intensity · Frequency · Pitch and tone · Temperature and humidity · Projection ·
Visual projection · Movement · Use of still photographs · Furnishing · Features · Play
objects · Mobiles · Play sculpture

Fig. 12

61

There is no doubt that in all buildings, service needs and performance are forming an increasingly important part and it may be worth keeping in mind the possibility that in the future, total testing facilities devised on a laboratory basis may form part of the building group.

Sheltered, semi-outdoor areas—planning

Outdoor play facilities should be tempered by good windbreaks and a substantial amount of sheltered play area. This can be achieved in various ways. One of the easiest might be a form of covered verandah-type structure forming an extension to classrooms, which would have the added advantage of protecting the windows of the main room from the build-up of solar heat and the heavy winter heat losses which so often occur.

Wherever covered facilities are provided, care must be taken to ensure that adequate wall shelter is provided as well as roof cover, so that the covered play area does not become a wind tunnel.

Outside facilities usually include a fairly large tarmac area and a similar or larger area of grass, permitting play and especially ball games under various ground conditions. Tarmac should be open in texture and well drained, and gritty surface dressings avoided.

Any shrubs or trees which may be used should be extremely strong and hardy. As a perimeter hedge they may be useful but architectural "landscape" type planting serves no purpose and is unlikely to last long.

Pools

A pool in which children can actually paddle serves a useful purpose. Outdoor paddling pools create great interest and the children usually love them, which of course enables the teacher to start from a point of interest. Water play of any sort is something in which many handicapped children are very interested. Such pools are usually only 150-200 mm (6-8 in) deep, carefully tiled and with round corners. Any stepping stones or similar features should be very carefully detailed to avoid accidents.

Pools may be rectangular, circular, free-shaped or indeed any shape which seems appropriate to the situation. To the child the first requisite is that it should contain water and that he or she is permitted to paddle.

Indoor pools, including "swimming pools" are also sometimes provided and have a definite therapeutic value. Some comment has already been made on these in the previous chapter. "Swimming pools" is perhaps a misleading term as the water is not more tha 0.75-1.0 m (2 ft 6 in to 3 ft) deep. Such pools are fully enclosed, usually up to 9.0 by 4.5 m (30 ft by 15 ft) in size, and of even depth throughout. They are used under supervision by juniors and seniors usually for one-hour periods or slightly less and often have a calming effect on disturbed children as well as helping to co-ordinate movements and provide new interests. A small number, in fact, actually learn to swim.

WATER PLAY

PADDLING AND PLAYING IN WATER

This applies mainly to nursery and special care groups

Siting · Close to building · Allows ease of supervision · Free and informal use · Nearness to towels, drying facilities, shoes, shelter and rest

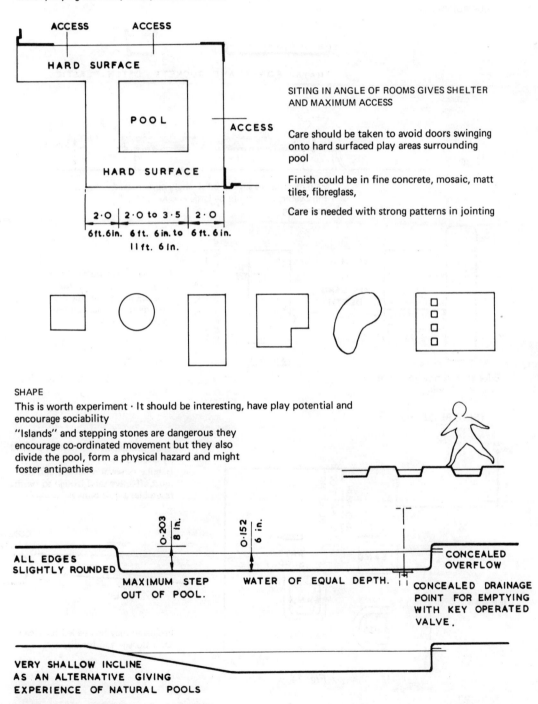

SITING IN ANGLE OF ROOMS GIVES SHELTER AND MAXIMUM ACCESS

Care should be taken to avoid doors swinging onto hard surfaced play areas surrounding pool

Finish could be in fine concrete, mosaic, matt tiles, fibreglass,

Care is needed with strong patterns in jointing

SHAPE

This is worth experiment · It should be interesting, have play potential and encourage sociability

"Islands" and stepping stones are dangerous they encourage co-ordinated movement but they also divide the pool, form a physical hazard and might foster antipathies

VERY SHALLOW INCLINE AS AN ALTERNATIVE GIVING EXPERIENCE OF NATURAL POOLS

PROFILES FOR POOLS   *Fig. 13*   63

SAND PLAY

AT ITS SIMPLEST THIS IS A SUBSTITUTE FOR SOIL
Children enjoy digging and filling receptacles · Tactile feel · Running through hands · Mixing
with water · More plastic possibilities

This applies mainly to nursery and special care groups

INSIDE BUILDINGS

TRAYS BOWLS AND BUCKETS OFTEN PLASTIC

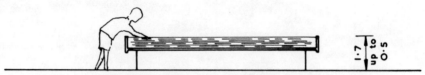

Main receptacles should be strongly constructed,
immovable and should be large enough to be
interesting

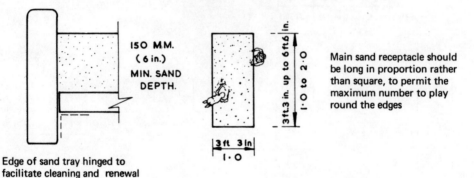

150 M.M.
(6 in.)
MIN. SAND
DEPTH.

Main sand receptacle should
be long in proportion rather
than square, to permit the
maximum number to play
round the edges

Edge of sand tray hinged to
facilitate cleaning and renewal

OUTSIDE BUILDINGS

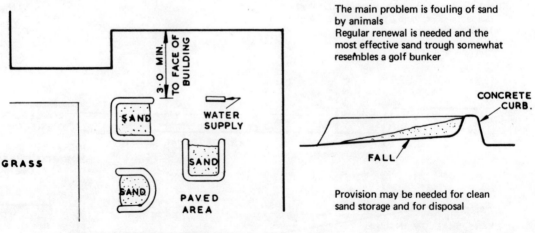

The main problem is fouling of sand
by animals
Regular renewal is needed and the
most effective sand trough somewhat
resembles a golf bunker

GRASS

3·0 MIN.
TO FACE OF BUILDING

SAND

WATER
SUPPLY

SAND

SAND

PAVED
AREA

CONCRETE
CURB.

FALL

Provision may be needed for clean
sand storage and for disposal

Fig. 14

64

WATER PLAY

3 TYPES — Playing with water
Paddling — Playing IN water
Immersion — Swimming pool

WATER PLAY AREAS · MOSTLY IN SPECIAL CARE UNITS AND NURSERIES

Basic need is for table tops at various levels with supply of water and vessels of different shapes and sizes

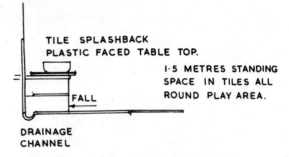

TILE SPLASHBACK
PLASTIC FACED TABLE TOP.

1·5 METRES STANDING
SPACE IN TILES ALL
ROUND PLAY AREA.

FALL

DRAINAGE
CHANNEL

Area is usually sited near other water play but not near sand

Vessels are plastic, non-buckling
Ordinary kitchen ware is very useful

At its simplest, water play requires only a bowl of water and one other vessel

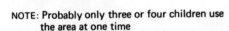

0·1 CLEARANCE

1·5	0·6
4 ft. 11 in.	2 ft. 0 in.
14 ft. 0 in.	13·0

PLAN OF TYPICAL
WATER PLAY AREA

NOTE: Probably only three or four children use the area at one time

ACTIVITIES Splashing hands in water
Filling receptacles
Pouring water from one vessel to another
Squirting water
Making bubbles
Using taps

PURPOSE Attraction of interest
Encouragement to play
Training with taps

Fig. 15

ADVENTURE PLAY

Outdoor or semi-outdoor, using simulated natural features · Indoor, using portable equipment (see 'halls')

Object · To arouse interest, develop imagination and foster self-reliance

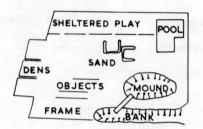

TYPICAL LAYOUT FOR ADVENTURE PLAY.

THE DESIGNER NEEDS TO USE HIS IMAGINATION IN DEVISING PLAY-OBJECTS AND PLAY SITUATIONS.

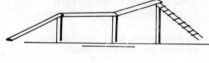

STEPS FORMED OF LOGS CEMENTED ON END OF LARGE STONES.

SLIDE   RAMP

A NATURAL SLOPE IS IDEAL.

ARTIFICIALLY FORMED MOUNDS WITH 'BRIDGE'.

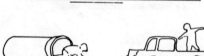

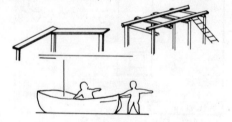

Tree trunks are useful, especially if they lead somewhere

Examples of adventure play features using timber, concrete, and disused equipment · Objects must not be too 'difficult' or dangerous but children usually attempt only the obstacles they think they can manage safely

Den or outdoor 'Wendy house'

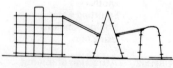

Example of portable climbing frames for outdoor or indoor use

Fig. 16

66

18. OPEN AIR CLIMBING FRAME AND EQUIPMENT, JUNIOR SCHOOL, GLOUCESTER

Other equipment and features

Outdoor sand play is another activity which seems to interest the younger children. Sand is often provided in "pits" formed by building small curb walls. It should be capable of regular and frequent renewal however, and not all teachers like this arrangement since it is liable to fouling by animals. An arrangement of portable sand trays, usable either inside or outside the building may in fact be preferable.

Climbing frames and similar equipment are useful, though again, thought, care and imagination must be used in providing them. For example, they must be sufficiently noticeable and complex to arouse interest but not to cause discouragement or danger. They must not be too high—1.80 m (6 ft) is quite high enough and they should be placed on soft ground in case of falls.

Swings are quite popular, though again, care must be taken to prevent other children wandering into the danger area when they are in use.

Adventure features are well worth providing. Suitably modified tree trunks, large diameter pipes, blocks, simulated railway engines and even old cars (again, suitably modified) provide real interest and the necessary stimulation to the child's imagination which may bring him to take an interest in something whereas he was previously totally disinterested.

Residential needs

The largest volume of accommodation in residential units will consist of bedrooms. In the main, children sleep in rooms containing four to six beds. Large dormitories are no longer used, though hospital units still form dormitories of up to twelve or fourteen beds.

The scale is essentially domestic in character and each child has a single bed, a locker and in fact as many features as can reasonably be provided to give him his own personal environment. This is considerably helped if the room has more than four corners, either by being structurally L-shaped or similar, or by a space-divider type of furniture arrangement.

Small single bedrooms are provided for dealing with children who are particularly noisy and disturbed or who find it especially difficult to sleep.

A small bedroom is also provided as a sick bay, though this is usually only for mild cases.

Bathrooms and W.C.s are provided usually in the form of facilities serving a group of children, so that a room is likely to be provided containing a small number of wash basins, say three or four, together with perhaps two W.C.s and an inner bathroom to serve two bedrooms with a total of twelve children.

The supervisor lives on the premises, together with a small number of staff who each have their own bedroom. Staff toilets and bathroom are separate. Eating facilities have already been described.

During working days, although the children are at a day centre or a sheltered workshop, facilities are needed for leisure time. A lounge may be planned either separately or in pair with a dining room. Some children spend a large amount of time just sitting, but these are the difficult minority and many others begin to take an active interest in games and hobbies. Ideally, a quiet lounge and a games room should be provided, one for quiet games, reading, painting and perhaps television, the other being for table tennis and noisy pursuits generally. The scale and planning is similar to that of the living room in an ordinary house, with allowance for a certain increase in size due to increase in numbers.

Again, free shapes are well worth considering, either formed by the structure or by the fittings and furniture and a small number of sheltered corners may be of value.

Apart from the wardens own flat, a small office will be needed near the main entrance for administrative purposes and for interviews and supervision.

Externally, it will be necessary to provide a small number of garages for permanent staff.

Some very interesting experiments have been carried out in which small groups of children live in what are virtually small bungalows, with only slightly extended sleeping facilities, so that children live eight or ten to a bungalow. This is about as near as it is possible to get to actual "home" conditions, though the strain on staffing must be considerable.

Educationally subnormal schools—criteria

These are not strictly within the scope of this book. Although the dividing line may be obscure between the weakest of children at an E.S.N. school and the best of children at a Junior Training School, mentally handicapped children are weaker in capacity than those at the school for the educationallly subnormal.

Sheltered workshops—criteria

These are usually sited near an Adult Training Centre and exist for the benefit of adults and adolescents who show themselves suitable for work but unready to venture out to normal work-places.

The buildings usually comprise a single, large indoor workshop up to about 120 m² (1 250 ft²) in area and are used for a very wide variety of work. One or two smaller subsidiary workshops of about 40 m² (450 ft²) maximum, are also provided of which at least one is used for female labour. Workshops should be adaptable and capable of being planned and replanned by varying the layout of benches and fittings. A good deal of manual and craft work and assembly of components is carried on generally with the use of jigs. The possibility of working out of doors in good weather should not be overlooked.

Large store rooms are needed for items awaiting assembly and for finished goods awaiting despatch. Double doors are needed to these store rooms and clearance height is important since fully assembled products may be quite large and unwieldy. The ratio of storage to work space is as high as 30 per cent. A 4 m (12-13 ft) minimum ceiling height is advisable, and good lighting and ventilation are essential.

Patients have their midday meal at the workshops and a dining area is required. As meals are usually brought in from central kitchens, especially when the workshops are attached to other buildings, a small servery for reheating and washing up is required.

Toilets and changing facilities are provided for patients and staff.

HEATING SERVICES

Most activity rooms need an even temperature of 65°-70° F. A separate boiler room is required, reached from outside the building and with good security.

OUTPUT: Working temperatures are about 5° F hotter than for normal domestic work.
Heavy demand on hot water and constant supply is needed for laundry in special care and nurseries.

CONTROL: Maximum automatic control to minimise staffing.
Peaks are likely to occur in demand about 10-12 a.m. and 2-4 p.m.

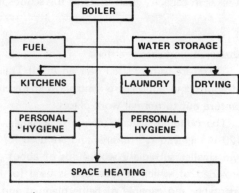

 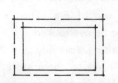 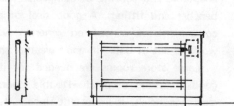

RADIATORS—If un-cased, these should be wall-mounted · Flush panel types are preferable · Space at back is recommended · Strong wire mesh guards or similar protection should be used.

Cased convector heaters are suitable.
Controls should be concealed whenever possible.
Key-operated hinged flap in casing or controls at back of casing might be used.

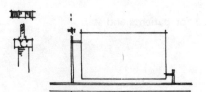

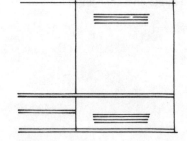

A simple security measure for un-cased heaters is to omit valve caps and retain a detached valve key for staff use.

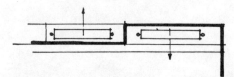

Overall — skirting heating

Fine mesh grille outlets are preferable to slatted or louvre outlets.

Convector heaters cased, serving two adjoining rooms.
Grilles integrated with and part concealed by shelf fitting.

Fig. 17

70

CHAPTER 5

Services

Introduction

Services in buildings for the mentally handicapped require special considera-tion and, as with so many other features, the normal criteria influencing choice and design do not necessarily apply.

There is much scope for enquiry and research in this field and it may be that requirements will be entirely reassessed in the future. So far, it has been assumed, perhaps incorrectly, that services such as heating, lighting, ventilation, and the supply of hot water, are roughly similar to those of any other building. In fact it does not follow that comfort conditions for mentally handicapped children are the same as those for normal children.

Requirements need to be assessed from two points of view—firstly the needs of the children themselves and secondly the exercising of control by the staff—as well, of course, as the actual comfort requirements of the staff. Control and flexibility in performance are both important aspects of services and the installation, in particular the various fittings, require very careful selection and detailing.

Heating

Most buildings require constant space heating and are therefore centrally heated.

The commonest type of installation appears to be an oil-fired boiler, though this must be viewed in the light of local conditions, availability of other fuels and the likely capital cost and running costs prevailing in the area at the time.

Most units have a caretaker/handyman who is responsible for the heating installation but he may only be employed part time and the hours of labour needed to maintain the boiler installation are therefore an important considera-tion. The use of time switches and thermostats or a compensator will save labour but these controls must be correctly positioned and set if the results are to be satisfactory.

The boiler size depends on the size of the building but in any case it will be situated in a separate boiler house with outside access, and good security arrangements are very important.

The calorifier is sometimes used to provide heat to a drying room for linen but it should be remembered that if this arrangement is adopted the heat output is not controllable and there will be a substantial amount of heat lost whether the drying room is in use or not. On the whole it seems preferable to keep the calorifier as part of the main heating installation and to have a separate drying room with heating coils which can be valved and the supply of heat regulated as required.

In terms of space heating the main need is for general warmth and a comfortable atmosphere throughout the whole of the building. The temperature should be a little higher than that regarded as comfort termperature for other purposes, say between 65° and 70°F (18° and 21°C). This is due to several needs. Firstly, there are likely to be non-ambulant cases or even cot cases in nurseries and special units and these will always require a higher room temperature due to their inability to move about. Secondly, a number of ambulant children are far from strong physically and are very susceptible to colds and especially to draughts.

Thirdly, many of the buildings are single-storey structures and the very spread-out horizontal form of plan inevitably leads to a large proportion of the walls being external. Present day construction will ensure that these are adequately insulated but the potential for heat loss is considerable, especially if the prevalence of large areas of window glazing is also borne in mind. Use of natural ventilation in the form of opening windows also accounts for a considerable heat loss.

Wall and floor surfaces should be reasonably warm since many children are likely to lean against walls and particularly to sit on floors. Unduly cold floors are prone to lead to incontinence which is particularly regrettable if it occurs at a time at which the child may be slowly but consistently learning cleaner habits.

Heat distribution is most commonly by means of a low-pressure hot water system with radiators of convector type blowing a low-velocity stream of warm air into the room at selected points. Normal hot water radiators are not particularly to be recommended since there is a greater-than-average risk of children burning themselves. Reactions to danger or discomfort are not necessarily as quick as in ordinary children and physical handicap might render the child actually unable to move quickly out of contact.

Even convector radiators present unexpected problems. For example, the normal type of convector radiator has outlet grilles either at the top and bottom of the vertical casing or in the horizontal surface of the top. Children may spend hours carefully poking various objects and materials into these grilles until the radiator casing is completely filled. Even normal children may put an occasional object into radiators but it must be remembered that behaviour in mentally handicapped children is often repetitive and obsessive. Thus they may take actual pleasure in the disappearance of objects through the grille; they may derive satisfaction from the actual physical deftness of being able to force things through the grille, and being told to stop doing so will either frustrate them or make them more determined. Whatever the pattern of behaviour or reason for it, the radiator will not function properly — this has been a very common experience.

Likewise, the presence of lever controls, knob controls, valves and similar gadgets on heating fittings leads to trouble. It is only normally child-like that such controls should be mis-used. Usually any detachable or un-screwable knob or cap disappears at a very early stage. In a way this at least shows the child is taking an interest in something! It is preferable for heating fittings to be built-in, either by incorporating them in partition walls, or in cupboard ranges or similar concealable fixtures.

A fine mesh is preferable to slots or grilles at the inlets and outlets; any controls should be either concealed within the casing, or difficult of access or complex in operation so that only the staff are able to adjust them. There should not be space behind heaters which can collect dust and which forms inaccessible caches of small toys, books, pencils, and pieces of paper.

High-level radiant panels, which leave the whole of the lower wall space free and are themselves safely out of reach are a worthwhile alternative.

Underfloor heating may seem at first to provide a good solution to the warming of the building fabric, but this is questionable since the heat may be too concentrated and would not give comfortable conditions if children sit on the floor. At the same time it again leaves wall spaces free and has no control problems.

As an alternative, evenly distributed low-level heating such as skirting heating is worth considering. Space heating is required to the whole area of the building, including toilets, and especially circulation spaces. There is considerable movement of people within the building and the number of air changes is therefore great.

The desirability of keeping the layout of the available space as flexible as possible and any variations of this layout should be borne in mind when designing the heating system. Again this suggests that an overall low-level method of heat distribution may be best. Pipe work wherever it occurs should be concealed, built-in, ducted or as a last resort, run at high level.

Bedrooms and lounges have the normal domestic requirements as regards heating with the proviso that a slightly higher-than-usual temperature is likely to be required, up to about 21°C (70°F).

Hot and cold water services—plumbing and fittings

Comment has already been made on the planning of toilet areas which are more open and prominent than in other buildings. Although from a normal building point of view it is regarded as economical—and therefore good practice—to concentrate and group plumbing fittings, this is only possible here to a limited extent. The most important consideration is that the fittings should

F

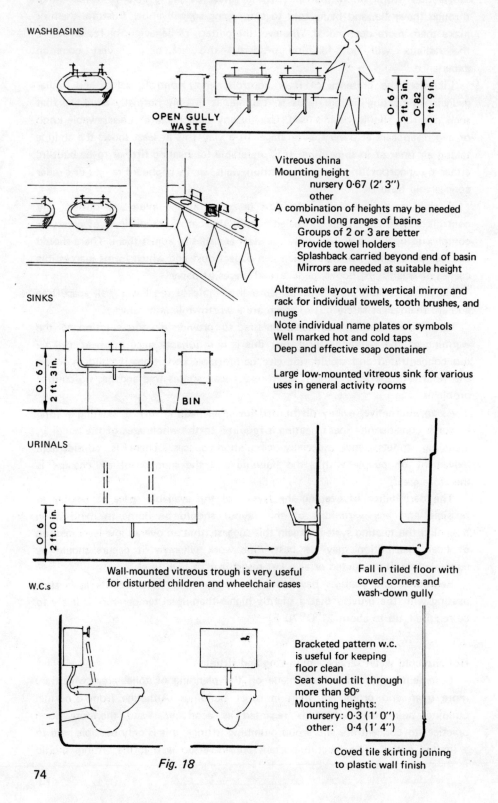

WASHBASINS

OPEN GULLY WASTE

0·67 2 ft. 3 in.
0·82 2 ft. 9 in.

Vitreous china
Mounting height
    nursery 0·67 (2' 3")
    other
A combination of heights may be needed
    Avoid long ranges of basins
    Groups of 2 or 3 are better
    Provide towel holders
    Splashback carried beyond end of basin
    Mirrors are needed at suitable height

Alternative layout with vertical mirror and rack for individual towels, tooth brushes, and mugs
Note individual name plates or symbols
Well marked hot and cold taps
Deep and effective soap container

Large low-mounted vitreous sink for various uses in general activity rooms

SINKS

0·67 2 ft. 3 in.

BIN

URINALS

0·6 2 ft. 0 in.

Wall-mounted vitreous trough is very useful for disturbed children and wheelchair cases

Fall in tiled floor with coved corners and wash-down gully

W.C.s

Bracketed pattern w.c. is useful for keeping floor clean
Seat should tilt through more than 90°
Mounting heights:
    nursery: 0·3 (1' 0")
    other: 0·4 (1' 4")

Coved tile skirting joining to plastic wall finish

Fig. 18

serve the needs of the children and of the staff in their work of care and teaching, and therefore fittings requiring plumbing may be quite widely dispersed.

Basins and W.C.s in nursery units are of the same small type as employed in ordinary nursery schools. The number of fittings in a range, however, is less, bearing in mind the need to keep the scale as "domestic" as possible. Hot and cold water services are required to wash-basins and a splash-back with carefully detailed junctions will be needed.

In day centres the junior and senior toilet and washing areas make use of normal sized fittings. It is difficult to generalise regarding mounting height of basins, though the height is likely to be between 685-787 mm (2 ft 3 in and 2 ft 9 in). Basins in junior sections may be mounted slightly lower than in senior but as there may quite easily be some very large children in junior classes and some quite small children in senior, a dual mounting height would be desirable. Furthermore, any attempts to design to conventional ideas of "junior" and "senior" requirements may render it more difficult for the staff to change arrangements and achieve the high degree of flexibility in use which is a desirable feature of these buildings.

W.C. sets usually have a high-level cistern. There is no particular argument against the use of low-level cisterns except that the mechanism is more easily tampered with and odd objects introduced into the cistern. If a high-level type is used the cisterns should have covers to prevent anything being thrown into them. Concealed cisterns built into ducts are over-elaborate and reminiscent of extreme institutional detailing and are not needed.

Adjoining the W.C. area a sluice room may be provided and this is a particularly useful feature in the nursery and in special care units. Small children often receive initial "pot training" and emptying, washing and sterilising facilities are needed in the form of a slop sink and a large Belfast sink with a copious supply of hot and cold water. Some establishments use disposable pot linings.

Reference has already been made to the need for baths or showers for dealing with some of the more difficult children, usually in the nursery stage but also in Special Care at all ages, and in some permanent residential centres where disturbed children form a part of the population. Architects appear to have given a lot of thought to these requirements but the results have been very ineffective and in some cases actually harmful. Opinion amongst staff varies as to whether a shower or bath is preferable.

If a bath is installed it should preferably be free-standing on three sides — a type with hand grips is useful.

Opinion is sometimes voiced that the bath should be raised so that staff do not have to bend over the child. Raising the bath however makes it very difficult to get some children into the bath at all, especially those who are physically handicapped. Also it is undesirable to put the child on a sort of raised dais. A type of arrangement in which a bath with low sides and handgrips is placed free standing in an area of floor space, with the floor lower by say 200 or 225 mm (8 or 9 in) at one side, might overcome most of the problems. It is important

SPECIAL UNITS

BATHS

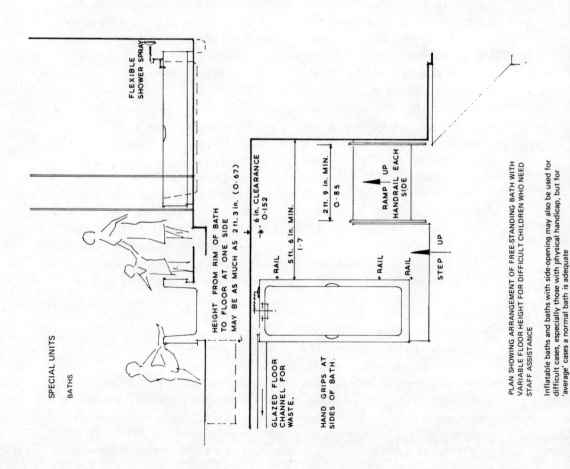

FLEXIBLE SHOWER SPRAY

HEIGHT FROM RIM OF BATH TO FLOOR AT ONE SIDE MAY BE AS MUCH AS 2 ft. 3 in. (0·67)

6 in. CLEARANCE 0·152

5 ft. 6 in. MIN. 1·7

2 ft. 9 in. MIN. 0·85

RAMP UP
HANDRAIL EACH SIDE

RAIL
RAIL
RAIL
STEP UP

GLAZED FLOOR CHANNEL FOR WASTE.

HAND GRIPS AT SIDES OF BATH.

PLAN SHOWING ARRANGEMENT OF FREE-STANDING BATH WITH VARIABLE FLOOR HEIGHT FOR DIFFICULT CHILDREN WHO NEED STAFF ASSISTANCE

Inflatable baths and baths with side-opening may also be used for difficult cases, especially those with physical handicap, but for 'average' cases a normal bath is adequate

TOILETS · W.C.s

NEEDS · Special care and nursery units

These require low mounted w.c. in wide compartment with helpful cues · Good laundry and drying facilities needed

Junior/Senior Residential or day school Physical handicap

Normal arrangements · Minor aids

Minimal laundry facilities

Special planning aids

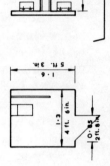

TWO TYPICAL LAYOUTS FOR NURSERY UNITS

ADULTS ROUTE
CHILDRENS ROUTE
COATS
TO ACTIVITY SPACE

NURSERY 1·5 / 4 ft.10½ in.
JUNIOR 1·75-2·0 / 5 ft. 8 in.
SENIOR 2·0 / 6 ft. 6 in.

Partitions and doors adjusted in height according to age group · Doors should be clearly distinguishable either by colour, by break in line of partitioning or by fittings . Indicators can be used but locks may be inadvisable

LINE OF APPROACH

DUCT

5 ft. 3 in. / 1·6

'Island' w.c. positions for physical handicap and disturbed cases

Duct and wing walls 2·0 (6' 6") high

5 ft. 3 in. / 1·6
1·3 / 4 ft. 6 in.
0·85 / 2 ft. 8 in.

Wide w.c. compartment for wheelchair cases
PLAN

76

that the installation should appear ordinary and homelike or the child may easily develop an aversion and become even more disturbed. There are instances in which designers, no doubt with the best of intentions, have provided a Terrazzo "washing slab" on a dais raised about 450 mm (18 in), combined with a large drainage fall and a sunken W.C. orifice. Such contraptions closely resemble a sacrificial slab and it requires little imagination to conceive that this may not be the best arrangement for disturbed children!

Where showers are used a flexible handset is the best type of fitting. A thermostatically controlled mixing valve will avoid accidents. Such a shower fitment is only used by staff for washing an individual child when needed. A shallow dished tray is provided and if this is sunk into the floor rather than provided with an upstand curb it will be much easier to use for physically handicapped cases.

Shower fitments for self use, even thermostatically controlled, should only be installed in senior establishments and only where the occupants have well developed abilities. On the whole baths are preferable.

Taps are of a normal pattern though hot and cold should be easily recognisable. A pattern in which the heads have different colours is good for this purpose. Ordinary capstan head taps are quite satisfactory and there is no need for the use of concussive taps or other allegedly "fool proof" types. A certain amount of water will be wasted but not more than in an ordinary school and it should be remembered that there is a high degree of supervision.

In any case, fittings and equipment should be as ordinary and as usual as possible.

The children do not need special types of equipment. The more they encounter everyday situations, and the more staff show confidence that the children will be able to deal with their surroundings, the more this situation generally comes about, and the children gain tremendously in self-confidence in the process.

Care should be taken that the hot-water supply is not scaldingly hot, and thermostatic control is useful. Single taps giving pre-mixed water to a selected temperature are not very useful as they preclude cold water for brushing teeth and do not aid in self-reliance.

Ordinary plug fittings are also used rather than any special type of built-in stopper. Basins must have a good overflow.

It is often found to be an advantage if overflows and wastes discharge into either a floor channel or a circular floor gully. This is hardly an arrangement to be encountered in the average home in England, but it serves several very useful purposes and is worth consideration. One of the main advantages is that it enables the floor to be washed down quickly and cleanly, a matter of considerable importance at times.

A further advantage is that it prevents any accidental flooding of the building. Despite the provision of overflow it is not entirely unknown for taps to be left on with basins already full, to an extent where water finds its way into other parts of the building.

Bathrooms in hostels require little comment since the criteria already applied to fittings elsewhere apply equally to this type of building. For juniors and seniors alike the bathroom and toilet layout and fittings should be as reasonably domestic as possible, and it is better to have a distribution of facilities, so that, for example, a bathroom and a small range of wash basins is provided for each group of children occupying two or three bedrooms, rather than that all the fittings should be grouped together in a large toilet block in the interests of economy.

Only in the case of very young children, unusually disturbed or maladjusted children, or cases of severe physical handicap, are special fittings likely to be necessary.

A laundry room is essential in hostels and a small laundry room is also an asset in day centres. Where facilities for boarders and day children are combined and especially in Special Units a laundry is absolutely vital. A sluice will be needed for dealing with fouled clothes and sheets in residential establishments, together with a couple of large deep sinks and a copious supply of hot and cold water. Container trolleys are used for soiled clothing and linen. A heavy duty washing machine is needed together with two normal or one larger capacity dryer, ironing and airing facilities; the two latter may possibly be separate and provided as an extension of a linen storage room. The volume of washing handled will vary to some extent according to school holidays—during which many day centre children are at their own homes—whilst some hostel residents may only attend from Monday to Friday or stay for short periods of from two to six weeks

In small day units, a foul sluice and a small washer/dryer are sufficient. A wet bag container service to a central laundry might be used in smaller hostels.

Linen stores are used for spare clothing, both top clothes and underclothes, as well as sheets, blankets, pillow cases, towels and bed linen. Slatted racks are needed and provision for labelling is useful. Although the children bring their own clothes, suitably labelled, a certain amount of interchange is inevitable due to the large numbers involved and labelling is sometimes of a general type such as "Vests—Small Boys", "Vests—Large Boys", etc. It is far better however, if each child has a "pigeon hole" in the linen room with his or her own name and personal clothes.

Ironing has already been mentioned as a need and the designer should remember that it may be necessary to "air" clothes by hanging them on rails after ironing, in a gently warm atmosphere.

The atmosphere in the laundry room itself becomes very damp and steamy and condensation may be troublesome. Ventilation should be good and air extraction may be needed together with warm air heating capable of minimising the coldness of surfaces on which condensation usually takes place.

Ventilation

Reliance is placed on natural ventilation as far as possible both in the interests of economy and of "normality", to simulate small-scale home conditions. Care

TOILETS, LAUNDRY AND DRYING

MAINLY FOR NURSERY AND SPECIAL CARE

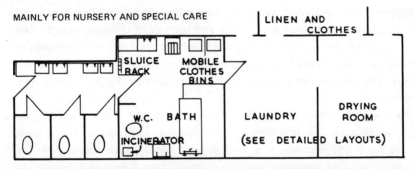

W.C.s
Special care, and nursery should have wide compartments, but one or two are sufficient for wheelchair use

LAUNDRY
Equipment · Based on 500/1000 articles per week · Mobile bins for soiled articles · Washing materials store · Sluice/sink for rough washing · Water softener if needed · Washing machines, say one large and one small or two heavy-duty domestic · Tumbler spin dryers, two 9/10 lbs capacity domestic pattern · Electric irons and boards · Racks · Mobile clothes trolly

DRYING

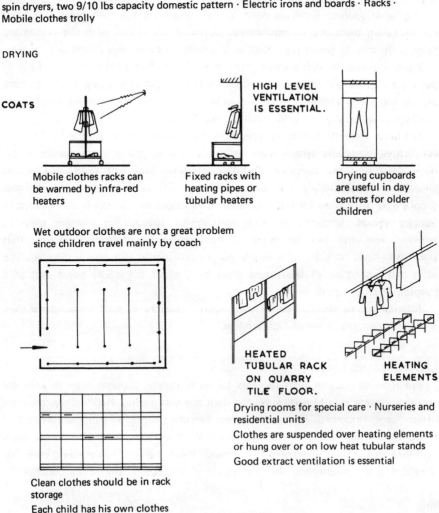

COATS

Mobile clothes racks can be warmed by infra-red heaters

Fixed racks with heating pipes or tubular heaters

HIGH LEVEL VENTILATION IS ESSENTIAL.

Drying cupboards are useful in day centres for older children

Wet outdoor clothes are not a great problem since children travel mainly by coach

HEATED TUBULAR RACK ON QUARRY TILE FLOOR.

HEATING ELEMENTS

Drying rooms for special care · Nurseries and residential units

Clothes are suspended over heating elements or hung over or on low heat tubular stands

Good extract ventilation is essential

Clean clothes should be in rack storage

Each child has his own clothes space properly labelled

Fig. 20

79

should be taken to avoid draughts and the designer should help staff by making the arrangements for ventilation as flexible as possible. The time of year, external weather conditions, room temperature, age and number of children, time of day, and type of activity are all important variables and the staff should be enabled to regulate the amount of ventilation and the position of open windows over a very wide range. The selection of windows with limited opening lights is a very false economy.

Due to the present day custom of designing rooms with a maximum of glass area, build-up of solar heat and glare are very common and tiresome phenomena. It may well be worth re-considering the design of rooms, according to their use, with a view to reducing somewhat the area of glass which is provided.

Windows with reasonably low cills will encourage the children to look at the outside world, provided that there is some interesting view or activity to be seen.

The most important activities and, one hopes, the most stimulating and interesting activities, are those which are taking place inside the room. Close linking of the room with the outside environment may even be a distraction at more senior levels. Glass placed too low may also be dangerous.

High-level opening windows need careful thought, since both poles and cords for operating them are unsatisfactory. Cords, in particular, with the customary brass ends, can be positively lethal, as the children swing them from side to side.

Window design as a component part of the building is dealt with more fully in the next chapter but in passing it is worth noting that in existing buildings there are far too many cramped high-level windows which do not provide satisfactory ventilation, especially in laundry rooms and kitchens.

Artificial ventilation may be needed in toilet areas as an auxiliary to natural ventilation, especially where these areas are reached via internal corridors and from classrooms and nurseries. Ordinary extractor fans with possibly a limited amount of local ducting are quite sufficient. Generally speaking the designer should aim to provide for cross-ventilation. Artificial ventilation is also needed in laundry rooms, kitchens, serveries and similar rooms. Air changes may be between five and ten per hour. It must again be stressed, however, that ventilation need only be of a simple nature provided it is properly planned. The scale and feeling of all the rooms must be that of a friendly home, not of a hospital or large hotel!

Internal rooms should not be used except possibly in staff areas where they will need appropriate ventilation services.

Lighting—natural light

Provision of natural light requires far more careful thought than it generally receives. Rooms should neither be too dark nor too glaring. Regrettably, they are often "over windowed". As a result they become distressingly brilliant at certain times of the day and with certain positions of the sun. A good external eaves overhang will help to overcome this, though there is also considerable ground for questioning the assumption that the whole of an external wall should necessarily

80

CARE SHOULD BE TAKEN TO ENSURE THAT WINDOWS ARE DOMESTIC IN SCALE AND FEELING AND GIVE AN EFFECT OF NORMALITY · TOO MUCH GLASS CAUSES EXCESSIVE GLARE AND BUILD-UP OF HEAT

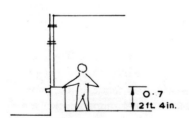

0·7
2 ft. 4 in.

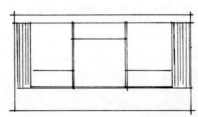

0·25 MAX.

AVOID SOLID WALL ABOVE WINDOW WHICH GIVES DARK AND OPPRESSIVE EFFECT.

Subdivision of windows should give flexibility in ventilation · At least 25% should be at high level

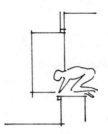

Pivot windows, top hung windows and side hung windows are all dangerous if there is a path outside

Large opening windows with low cills are also a hazard

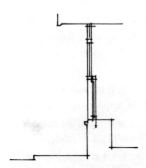

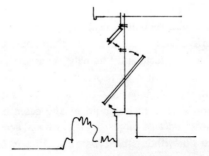

Windows which open outward should only be used with exterior flower beds or other non-walking areas

Horizontal sliding sashes are effective · Lower sash may be fixed · Overhanging eaves may prevent glare

Floor-to-ceiling glazing is often misleading · If used, the lower lights should be in wired glass Curtains are desirable · Blinds should not be used except possibly for roller, blackout blinds used in rooms for film projection

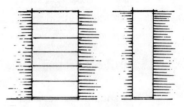

Avoid over-dramatic or misleading subdivisions or shape in fenestration

Fig. 21

be window. If it is, then there should be some easy way of closing sections off if required. Light should, however, be provided to the full height of the room to avoid an oppressive dark area above the window head.

Reference has already been made to the value of overhanging eaves in preventing glare and it may likewise be worth considering the provision of shade by means of an outside canopy or blind, possibly even a permanent visor formed of translucent plastic material. If the area outside the room is used as a sheltered play area this will also have the effect of protecting the inner room.

An attractive homely effect can be achieved by the use of curtains. These are essential in specifically residential buildings but can also be used to advantage in some circumstances in day centres. A plain coarse woven fabric is the most serviceable. Nylon track and runners are preferable to metal runners. They are slightly stiffer to operate and much quieter and are thus less likely to draw too much attention from the children. Inevitably, they will receive a certain amount of unorthodox use, but this is seldom excessive and the provision is well worth while. More sophisticated types of window protection such as venetian blinds and other spring blinds are not advisable!

In some circumstances, blackout arrangements may be needed for film display and television. This will apply in the more senior years at a Junior Training School, and similar arrangements may be needed in a large common room such as a hall used for general purposes including parent/teacher meetings.

There may be scope for a wider use of television and films at all levels and in all buildings than operates at present. Some of the children including the younger ones appear to be quite interested, but no systematic research has been carried out as far as is known.

High level and windows of elaborate or dramatic shape, proportion or design are not recommended, the former on account of their slightly claustrophobic effect and the latter for their obvious divergence from pleasantly small and personal scale and "homely" character.

Top light may prove necessary because of the large horizontal spread of some of the buildings and the deep plan shape which results. This applies to internal corridors (which should in any event be kept to a minimum) and possibly to the inner part of large rooms, farthest away from the external walls. It is preferable to do without this type of lighting as far as possible. Corridors, where they exist, are better lit by providing breaks in the plan so that windows can be used. The plan shape of rooms should be so devised that top light is not really necessary, as it otherwise provides a very awkward and inharmonious feature. This comment applies most strongly to main rooms and main circulation spaces though it is appreciated that it is, perhaps, impossible to avoid a certain amount of top lighting in other spaces such as toilet areas.

Artificial lighting

This should be as "natural" as possible in appearance. As with natural lighting, it should be very carefully planned to avoid both undue shadow and excessive brightness. This is not to say that there should be no variation in lighting; a certain reasonable degree of variation is in keeping with natural conditions, but it should be graduated and kept within average domestic limits. Deep shadow must be avoided. In addition, careful enquiry should be made as to the range of uses of any particular room or space and comfort conditions provided for both children and staff. As always the need for flexibility in plan layout is an important matter and this will have a bearing on the type of installation, the type of fittings and to some extent, the positions selected for them.

Intensity at a point about 900 mm (3 ft) above floor level should be 125-160 lumens per m² (12-15 lumens per ft²) for general rooms.

Tungsten lighting appears to be most satisfactory for general purposes at the present time. This is certainly true of residential spaces such as bedrooms, lounges and dining rooms and is also widely favoured for classrooms and other dayrooms.

The need for maximum flexibility in the use of day-spaces poses a problem however, and the designer can only "grid" the day-space with suitable tungsten fittings and hope for the best. It may be worth considering the use of low intensity luminated ceiling panels of a flush type, but as far as is known, no study has yet been made of the practical applications of this idea.

Fluorescent lighting is normal for kitchens and serveries. It is also sometimes used for classrooms but does not so far appear to have been used very effectively. In some cases it has been shielded by diffuser grilles which have cut down the level of lighting too much, while in others the appearance has been far too artificial, the effect being nearer to that of department store lighting than of a smallish pleasant room for a group of young children. It cannot be stressed too strongly that unless a deliberate and calculated experiment is being made, there is no room for conscious architectural effects and dramatic lighting decor in this type of building.

A normal type of switching arrangement is used, and provided a good quality flush switch of ordinary pattern is employed, there is no need for switches to be concealed or placed abnormally high on the wall. It is best if lights in a room are controlled by at least two switches so that the occupants have some warning if a child decides to play with the switches.

A lower, softer level of illumination is needed for bedrooms and low illumination night lights are used in corridors and circulation spaces in residential buildings.

All fittings should be of a pattern which is easily maintained and renewed, and for which replacements will not be too difficult to obtain.

Plastic lighting fittings are preferable to glass and this is especially true in halls and similar spaces where ball games are likely to take place. In the latter case it may well be worth considering the use of high mounted or even flush fittings to give the maximum possible volume of free and unobstructed space.

Likewise the designer should avoid using any lighting fitting of an open "trough" type into which objects can be thrown (which are usually very difficult to retrieve).

Above all, the designer must talk to staff and to medical and psychiatric experts and obtain the broadest possible picture of requirements, to which he must then add his own critical imagination. Only in this way is a satisfactory scheme likely to emerge.

As yet, very little experiment seems to have taken place, though undoubtedly, lighting can have a very important effect on environment. Variable mounting height, position, intensity and colour may all have a part to play. There appears to be no data on the effect of lighting nor on whether variation in the lighting might be appropriate according to age or the type and degree of disability or disturbance.

CHAPTER 6

Finishes

Although the importance of finishes can never be over emphasised, they are of exceptional significance in the design of buildings for the mentally handicapped, since together with planning and services, they make a very large contribution to the total environment. This total environment may be a child's main or even its sole surroundings—for years, maybe for life, and thus the designer has a very serious responsibility.

Like other parts of the total environment, the finishes are susceptible to assessment from two different standpoints, that of the patients and that of the staff. Neither can be said to be paramount. It is sometimes argued that the children are not particularly observant of environment and are capable of being happy or unhappy under almost any conditions. Even if this was true (and the author considers that it is not true) the same could not be said of the staff. Attacking the problem from a slightly different standpoint therefore, it is important to create surroundings in which the staff are happy and in which they are stimulated to creative work and thought. Only in this way can the children receive the most effective attention.

Criteria

Some of the criteria are those which would normally be attached to the design of almost any building and some are less well known. Both categories are listed, though not necessarily in order of importance.

Appearance

Quite obviously, the appearance should be pleasing. It is necessary, however, to look a little deeper. The appearance should be acceptable and pleasing to both staff and children and considerable imagination will need to be exercised in judging what is pleasing to the children. The question of colour is examined in detail at another point in this book.

Finishes may have an appearance of being hard or soft, dull or shiny, dark or light, sparkling or matt, porous or impervious, "warm" or "cold", cheerful or forbidding and many other things. To an impressionable child, these attributes may have great importance. It is impossible to select in a manner which pleases everybody, especially when the patients are not known to the designer as people. Nevertheless, an exercise in imagination is called for and can help the designer to avoid the more obvious pitfalls. For example, a matt black surface often produces a forbidding effect. On walls and floors and especially around fittings, children tend to dislike it and thus to attach particular dislikes to a particular spot, such as a bath fitting or a toilet.

A crushing appearance in the shape or proportion of an element might possibly be used to reinforce a particular prohibition but can have very little real place in an environment in which the principal aim is to produce an atmosphere of warmth and light, of interest and love.

These requirements, at once simple and human and yet difficult to achieve will prohibit absolutely many formal effects and architectural conventions which designers tend to use without much deliberation.

A good general test of the validity of appearance is to question whether it would be acceptable under normal simple home surroundings.

A feature which passes this test will probably be acceptable to patients and staff alike.

Once accepted, appearance is very quickly reduced to something no longer noticed, though its effects will remain in the background and any feature which originally caused strong dislike will continue to be disliked.

Cost

This is of no concern to children or staff but of considerable importance to the local health authority, the financing body and the designer.

Capital cost limits are laid down for the buildings either in terms of an amount per ft^2 * of floor space or as an item of cost per place. This has a very definite bearing on the finishes which can be chosen, but if these finishes are reasonably domestic in character they are usually within the total cost limits.

Cost limits (quoted elsewhere) are currently within the range £5/6 per ft^2 and thus permit most normal finishes. Expensive wood panelling and elaborate board finished concrete are unsuitable!

Designers sometimes argue that an enlarged capital cost will produce a saving on maintenance and running costs, but whilst this may be true, most financing authorities are chiefly interested in the actual capital cost of the building.

Maintenance

This factor has a strong bearing on cost, though the close connection between the two is not always acknowledged by the authorities. Under this heading the designer should consider the questions of method and frequency of cleaning, of likely wear and tear and how well the finish will stand up to them.

The length of life of the finish should be considered and the method and cost of renewal or replacement.

* Presumably, this will be changed to an amount per metre^2 in the near future.

Some finishes permit small local renewals and repairs to be carried out and these are preferable to a finish requiring total renewal overall.

In general, a finish which can be renewed by an "overlay" is preferable to one which requires complete stripping or similar elaborate and costly preparation.

The designer needs to exercise his imagination in regard to the use the building will receive and the manner in which it will be operated.

Simple instances of this are the selection of finishes which will not harbour dust and dirt, and finishes which do not easily scratch or show dirty finger marks. Particular locations may receive exceptionally heavy use. This is generally noticeable on the threshold and immediately inside a room, at the edges of doors, notably round the door handle, against radiators and window catches, round lighting switches and at corners and edges of walls. In these situations, an extra hard-wearing finish is advisable. External corners of walls may have a metal or a plastic trim. Perspex shields are useful round switches.

It may be worth considering the use of a cheap finish, provided it is adequate, on the basis that it will be renewed at regular intervals, rather than using a better quality finish which lasts longer, but is not capable of amendment or alteration for a long period of time.

Variability

In a normal building, choice can be made from a confident knowledge of established facts. Buildings for the mentally handicapped are still in an experimental stage and the various features which make up the total environment should be as flexible as possible.

Finishes, no less than other aspects of the building, will be found to achieve varying results (or lack of results) and maximum variability is desirable.

This permits the changing of those factors which have been found particularly useful, and should be increased, and those which are particularly bad and need elimination.

Thus, a finish which permits easy change or replacement is always worth serious consideration.

An interesting variant is the type of finish, such as certain patterns of floor or ceiling tile or wallpaper, which has a different appearance when viewed under different lighting conditions or from different angles. Anything which might catch the children's interest is worth consideration and might have both educational and psychological value. Such finishes should, however, be used with discretion and not applied indiscriminately.

Impression

This is sometimes regarded as synonymous with appearance. There is however, an intangible difference—one very difficult to describe, but none-the-less important—in that appearance may be quite simply noted by the eye without any particular feeling or reaction whereas the creation of an impression goes considerably deeper. It may indeed be created not purely by the finishes but by a combination of factors and it may have a consistent, repetitive, and quite possibly a deep effect on the user of the building.

It can thus be produced by a combination of architectural shape and proportion, placing of solids and voids, lighting, temperature, and ventilation and choice of finishes especially in regard to their colour and texture.

Texture

The texture of finishes is important from two different points of view. For the staff the finishes should have a texture which will not retain dust and which can be easily cleaned with a minimum of effort. Something has already been said under the heading of "maintenance" concerning the likely effect of chalk, paint, pencils, and sticky fingers. On the other hand the selection of finishes which are uniformly hard, shiny and impervious, creates a hard mechanical and unsympathetic environment, and the aim therefore is to produce the necessary hard wearing properties but with a homely, warm and "comfortable" effect.

Whilst this is true as a general principle, there remains scope for a good deal of enquiry in regard to use of colour and texture. The children are often interested in the actual tactile feel of surfaces and substances. Anything which can be used to draw their interest may possibly lead to further communication with their teachers, and although the point may seem a small one, it assumes greater importance when considering these exceptional children and how they can be helped. Thus, it may be worth investigating the use of different textures at different points and locations within the building for the specific and positive purpose of attracting interest.

The acoustic properties of textured surfaces may also be important in controlling noise at specific points.

From the staff angle, it is necessary to cushion the staff rest-room as far as possible from the rumbustious life of the rest of the building. Staff dealing with the children have an exceedingly tiring and often very discouraging time and need an environment which is as comfortable and as restful as possible when they are not in direct contact with the children.

In this context, the finished texture can be used both to produce this impression and to absorb sound and provide peace.

The same is true, though to a lesser extent, in regard to the supervisor's room. This is the administrative centre of the building and although it is a purposeful workroom, the effect should be one of quietude, so that again textured finishes may be used to absorb unwanted sound, especially outside the room but in its immediate vicinity.

Performance factors

Under this heading, finishes should be assessed in relation to certain qualities which are of importance in all buildings and which need little comment. The principal of these are:

Thermal conductivity

Fire resistance

Resistance to flame spread

Sound resistance (where applicable).

Having examined the principal general criteria which operate in making selection of suitable internal finishes, these will now be applied to the consideration of finishes for various points within the buildings.

Entrance
Considerations

There should be an impression of welcome and optimism.

The entrance is used by both children and visitors.

Equipment and supplies are sometimes brought in by this route.

Children arriving are still in outdoor shoes or boots.

Approach is generally from a paved area outside.

The entrance is thus subject to extensive wear and tear.

It must be easily cleaned and maintained.

It must be kept warm and welcoming.

No one is likely to stop there long, but there will be constant traffic at peak times.

If possible it should have some directional quality.

Suggested solutions

Floor   Quarry tiles.

Wood blocks.

PVC tiles on screed.

A large area of door mat in recessed mat well should be provided at the entrance.

Walls   It is important that the walls should hide wear and tear and absorb noise and clatter from the hard floor finish.

Plaster and paint are usual in existing buildings but these are hard and noisy.

More texture is desirable.

This could be achieved by using paper backed vinyl or wallpapers (on the basis that they may need renewing fairly often).

Timber panelling—vertical or horizontal boarding—is worth considering, both for its warmth, its acoustic qualities and for the directional sense which can be obtained. Such effects must not be used too much however. Pinboards should also be considered.

The use of wall ornamentation such as pictures can give a semi-domestic feeling, and experimentation may be worthwhile. Ceramic or decorative tile panels are also effective.

Ceiling   Absorbent plaster. Acoustic tiles—if these are used, dramatic patterns should be avoided.

Emphatic architectural statements are not usually required in these buildings.

Cloak areas

These are specifically areas for hanging outdoor garments and for changing shoes. The space is loosely linked to the entrance area as a general rule but may be attached to dayrooms in some cases, not necessarily fully enclosed by partition walls to form a separate room.

Finishes should be cheerful and hard-wearing and should be capable of withstanding moisture, scraping and impact. The area should be warm, light, and well ventilated. Wall finishes should be capable of integration with rails, coat pegs, number or symbol plates, and other similar fittings and fixtures where these are wall mounted rather than mobile.

Suggested solutions

Floor   Quarry tiles.

PVC tiles.

Possibly thick linoleum.

Care must be taken that any floor finish used does not become slippery, either in itself or through frequent polishing or in wet weather.

Walls   Hard wall plaster—emulsion paint. Hard wall plaster with vinyl finish. Horizontal timber boarding (permitting integration of coat rails).

Ceiling   The light reflective properties are important.

Plaster and emulsion paint.

Ceiling tiles.

Toilets

Selection of suitable finishes will require a great deal of careful thought. Amongst staff and teachers and even children and parents, toilets can become something of a fetish with the result that instead of receiving insufficient consideration they receive too much.

Despite the important place they are allocated in the design process, the results are often not particularly good.

The finishes should produce an effect which is light, airy and pleasant and which is in no way gimmicky or over-played. Planning and the selection of fittings are both discussed elsewhere.

Finishes should be hardwearing and impervious. They must be capable of withstanding water, acids, detergents, and constant cleaning and the jointing must therefore be as effective as the selected material itself. The material should also be capable of looking reasonably fresh and new for a long period of time despite the heavy punishment it receives. If possible it should lend itself to coving at the junction with walls either by working of the material itself or by the use of special pieces or accessories.

Ideally, the material should also feel reasonably warm. The children are often susceptible to extremes of temperature and adversely affected by anything which is unduly cold or hot. A child given to feeling walls with his hands or abruptly sitting on the floor is likely to gain a bad impression of the whole toilet process if he finds the surfaces unpleasantly cold. At the same time, it is realised that this need conflicts with the previously stated requirements concerning hard wear and impervious surface, and the conflict of needs is difficult to solve satisfactorily with materials currently available.

The colour of surfaces may also have some importance, but this is discussed in another section.

Suggested solutions

Floor   Tile or mosaic used in conjunction with underfloor heating.

            "Jointless" vinyl flooring.

            Magnesium oxychloride jointless flooring.

Walls   Tile or mosaic—used in conjunction with heated floor.

            Matt-finish formica.

            Note: Whatever choice is made should give the toilets a personal and domestic scale. Thus large areas of terrazzo and large scale floor to ceiling tiling which give an institutional appearance should not be used.

Ceiling   Plaster and emulsion paint.

            Possibly anti-condensation paints.

Generally   Particular care is needed in detailing finishes around W.C.s, basins

91

19. CORNER OF A 'CLASSROOM' USED BY JUNIOR CHILDREN.
The sink is used for general classroom purposes. Note the changes in colour of floor tiles denoting areas for different purposes. The curtain is rather forbidding.

and other fittings. It is difficult to clean behind W.C.s and a pattern which is wall mounted is preferable from this point of view. There is no particular need to case-in the cisterns especially in view of the need for an average domestic appearance, but the design should be neat and well integrated with the finish.

Playrooms and classrooms

The two types of room are bracketed as there is little difference in the performance required from each and their use is similar.

The rooms are about the same size as normal classrooms but a great deal less formal in their layout.

Finishes should be serviceable, hard wearing, capable of easy renewal or replacement, warm and welcoming in appearance but not too obtrusive.

These are the rooms in which the children will spend a large part of their day and in which the maximum effort in teaching and training will be expended.

92

Great flexibility is therefore needed in the equipment and performance of the rooms which should act as a frame and a background to activities.

The basic finishes should be serviceable and simple, leaving equipment and adjustable factors to produce the stimulus to activity.

It is important that floors should be warm in the playrooms occupied by the smaller children, as they are prone to sitting on the floor and to crawling and similar floor activities.

Suggested solutions

Floor	PVC tiles. Heavy linoleum or vinyl. Cork tiles.	Classrooms and playrooms.
also	Wood blocks. Wood strip flooring.	Classrooms for older children (no floor activities).

Walls   Plaster and emulsion paint.

Extensive areas of pinboard and similar display are likely to be needed. There will also be cupboard ranges and the amount of unoccupied wall space will probably not be very large. Plastic laminated finishes on fittings are useful.

Ceilings   Light and reflective. Plaster and emulsion paints or suitable tile finish.

Storerooms

Stores are ancillary to classrooms and playrooms, each of which should have its own store.

Finishes are simple in character, especially as the rooms are only used by staff and possibly by older children.

Floors, walls and ceilings are generally an extension of finishes already used for the main rooms which they serve.

Practical rooms :

These rooms are used only by the older children and may cover a very wide range of activities. They are halfway between a senior classroom and a workshop and should provide stimulus, instruction and practice in various social and creative activities. The range of possibilities is so wide that in practice they vary enormously in value and in extent of use. The most likely demands on finishes are that they should be hard wearing, easily swept and cleaned, and form a suitably neutral background to many activities. These activities may include woodwork, cut-outs, model-making, weaving, painting and drawing, sewing, hairdressing and make-up, perhaps washing and cooking, and as many other things as the ingenuity of teachers and the estimated needs of older children can produce.

Specific activities such as washing or cooking are provided within a subsection and there is much to commend this since the demand made on the finishes is different.

Floors will need frequent sweeping, though not necessarily any other care. They are likely to receive a polish once a week, though cleaning staff should be dissuaded from too frequent polishing which can be dangerous.

Suggested solutions

Floors   PVC tiles.

Wood blocks.

Greaseproof PVC tiles in cooking and washing areas.

Walls   Plaster and paint.

Tiles to dado height in cooking and washing areas. Alternatively a matt finished laminated plastic could be used.

Ceilings   Plaster and paint.

Workshops

Most of the comments already made regarding practical rooms will apply to workshops, except that there is a greater intensity of use and the layout will include heavy benching rather than tables. Light machines, such as bending machines or presses are sometimes installed.

The context is not fully industrial but inclines in that direction, with a corresponding demand for hard wearing properties.

Only senior children are involved and workshops border on the province of adult training.

Apart from being hard wearing, finishes should be easily swept and cleaned and reasonably warm and cheerful. A light appearance is needed but visually they are subservient to the operations which are being carried out.

Suggested solutions

Floors   PVC tiles.

Wood blocks.

Possibly granolithic or quarry tiles for areas involving heavy machinery but these areas should be kept to the minimum.

Walls	Light and reflective.
	Plaster and paint.
	Some pinboard areas for displaying patterns, etc.
Ceilings	Plaster and paint.

Staff and admin. rooms

These require little comment as they relate to an ordinary and well-recognised use.

It is worth noting however, that staff rest rooms should be warm, comfortable, relaxing and "low in key".

The use of wallpaper or vinyl wall coverings on walls and carpet on the floor is therefore strongly recommended.

Halls and dining rooms

Finishes should be attractive and stimulating, capable of easy cleaning and not easily damaged by frequent scraping and impact of tables, chairs and other equipment.

A good deal of moving and re-arranging of furniture and heavy gear, large mats and equipment occurs. In combined rooms, for example, it will be necessary to set out tables for the midday meal and then clear them away for afternoon activities.

Suggested solutions

Floors	Wood blocks.
	Hardwood strip.
	PVC tiles.

Walls	Plaster and emulsion paint.	
	Vinyl wall coverings.	In both cases a dado or preferably a broad dado
	Ceramic tile wall panels and plastic laminates might be considered.	rail is recommended.

Ceilings	Light and reflection is needed.
	A variable acoustic performance is needed too. An impression of overwhelming clatter at meal times should be avoided and acoustic tiles may help here in cutting down the sound. If the hall has a stage, a separate sounding board or acoustic panel may be needed.

Lounges

In residential buildings the children need to relax and feel at home in the evenings and at weekends.

Junior and senior children will watch television, carry on hobbies, extend their learning/play activities such as painting and drawing, will sometimes listen to records and indulge in many of the activities carried on by ordinary children, though only patchily and to a varying extent of involvement and effectiveness.

Games such as table-tennis are also in use. Planning and layout of the lounge are considered elsewhere.

Finishes should be compatible with heavy use but as near as possible to those used in a personal home and with a certain degree of stimulation.

Suggested solutions

Floor	PVC tiles.	
	Wood blocks.	A considerable area to be covered by carpet and/or rugs, or carpet tiles
	Stained and polished boarding.	

Walls	Plaster and paint.
	Wallpaper.
	Vinyl papers.

Use of wall decoration in the form of pictures and mobiles should be considered.

Ceilings	Plaster and paint.

Dormitories and bedrooms

These vary in size from single rooms to rooms for ten or twelve, though six is a desirable maximum. Again, the effect should be as much like home as possible; simple, warm, pleasant finishes similar to those used in an ordinary bedroom should be used.

Children should be encouraged to develop a sense of their own identity. They like to feel they possess their own bed, their own corner, their own possessions.

Sweeping and cleaning by staff will have a modifying effect on what is possible.

Suggested solutions

Floor	PVC tiles.	
	Lino.	Small rugs or carpet squares in addition.
	Wood blocks.	

Walls	Plaster and emulsion paint.
	Wallpaper.
	Vinyl wall coverings.

Ceiling	Plaster and paint.

96

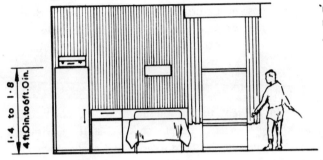

'PERSONAL CORNER'
FOR ONE CHILD IN
A SIX BED DORMITORY.

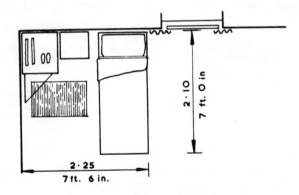

PLAN AND ELEVATION
SHOWING SUGGESTED
SLEEPING ARRANGEMENT
FOR ONE CHILD

Equipment:
Divan bed or hospital-type
bed (according to handicap)
Bedside locker
Hanging cupboard
Small rug or carpet
Headboard or shelf

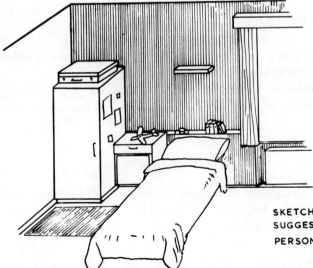

SKETCH SHOWING TREATMENT
SUGGESTED TO CREATE A
PERSONAL CORNER.

Fig. 22

Toilet areas

Residential toilet areas attached to sleeping accommodation are similar to those in ordinary houses.

Children in residential hostels usually have a reasonable amount of social awareness and there are thus no special requirements in regard to finishes which should be as far as possible like those in the ordinary home. The older child who remains antisocial will probably, alas, be in a hospital, where the conditions are somewhat different.

Circulation space

Corridors and lobbies should be kept to the minimum. In the day centre, circulation space is used by a large number of people, children, staff and visitors. Finishes should be warm, welcoming but also hard wearing and easily cleaned. If possible, they should also be quiet and mildly sound absorbent.

There may be a strong argument for using a dado or dado rail to prevent damage and unduly hard wear, but this idea must be viewed with caution as it could produce an impression of long corridor vistas by heightening the perspective.

Pattern and texture in the finishes can be used deliberately to give direction, to lead and to obviate any impression of undue length.

Suggested solutions

Floor   PVC tiles.

               Wood blocks.

               Cork tiles.

Walls   Plaster and emulsion paint.

               Vinyl wall coverings.

Note: In all cases, finishes should be specified which make a reasonable transition between the various rooms or spaces to which they give access.

A careful combination of materials should be selected which are complementary or contrasting (hard/soft, matt/glossy) and which will give a balanced solution.

Fittings and built-in furniture

Under the heading of fittings are included all those items which are fixed into the building which do not form part of the building structure. Apart from the more obvious fittings such as sanitary ware, there is great need for the use of built-in fittings of various kinds.

One of the first questions which must be decided is whether a large

CIRCULATION SPACE

PROBLEM – To minimise transit areas, especially corridors, and at the same time to avoid disturbance to rooms or spaces used for quiet activities

AVOID

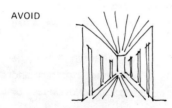

Corridor vistas, which are anonymous and disturbing, especially when there are many similar doors

When corridors are unavoidable, keep them short, reasonably wide (1·5, say 5' 0"), avoid 'vista patterns'

Breaks and recesses in the corridor wall can be used for minor activities and to give glimpses of the exterior

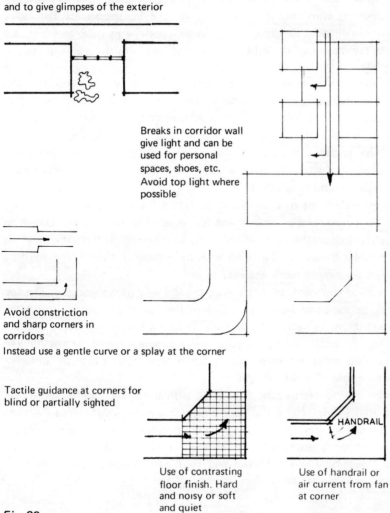

Breaks in corridor wall give light and can be used for personal spaces, shoes, etc. Avoid top light where possible

Avoid constriction and sharp corners in corridors

Instead use a gentle curve or a splay at the corner

Tactile guidance at corners for blind or partially sighted

Use of contrasting floor finish. Hard and noisy or soft and quiet

Use of handrail or air current from fan at corner

HANDRAIL

Fig. 23

proportion of the storage furniture should be movable or fixed since this will have an important effect on planning, on floor space requirements and on the construction of walls.

Built-in cupboards and storage furniture are safer, neater, more economical in space and usually more efficient. They are also more dust-free and make it easier to keep the rooms clean. At the same time they are less flexible in use, since they cannot be moved about.

Maximum flexibility in use is a very important consideration since the teaching and training process cannot follow a clearly predetermined pattern and methods may be changed quite suddenly as a result of experience or experiments.

Hence, cupboards, book shelves, worktops and display spaces should be designed to allow the maximum possible variation in arrangement and performance.

It may even be worth considering designing these fittings in such a way that they can be moved to another wall, or another position within the rooms and spaces, if desired. Such a scheme will require the fittings to be made in individual and self-supporting units and on a repetitive modular basis. Likewise, the rooms or play spaces will need designing to the same repetitive module, and provided this is done, the maximum flexibility can be combined with the maximum use of built-in fittings.

It must also be remembered that in common with every other aspect of the buildings, these fittings need design consideration from two distinct and often opposing view points, namely, that of the staff and that of the children.

At the junior level there is a difference in height, in reach, and in physical capacity. There is also a very definite difference in intelligence or its application.

Teaching and social training cover a wide, general field and many very simple operations may be used to advantage.

Getting something out of a cupboard or placing the right object on the right shelf may be a considerable achievement for some of these children. Failure to open a cupboard door when encouraged to do so may lead to frustration and set back. If "teaching-by-use" of this kind is to be employed, then fittings must be devised which are easy to reach and easy to use.

Low ranges of cupboards against walls provide a very useful worktop. The top surface may be varied in height according to the age of the children using the room. Sliding doors are less likely to cause accidents than swing doors, and are also less likely to sustain serious damage, but are more difficult for the children to operate. Cupboards are often distinguished from each other by different colours or by means of a cut-out symbol.

Blackboards in horizontal ranges mounted with the lower edge no more than about 380 mm (15 in) above the floor and with a small ledge below them are useful in rooms for young children. It is hardly possible to provide too much pin board space and many teachers favour this even for circulation spaces.

A large trough-type sink with hot and cold water mounted at a height the children can use is a great asset.

Rooms for younger children involve water and sand play, usually by means of large movable trays and bowls. Any attempt to incorporate permanent features is likely to prejudice flexibility in the layout of the room.

All sorts of teaching and adventure gadgets can be provided with the help of a little imagination. Even old telephone sets can be pressed into service. Mobiles are very popular. Straight lines for walking on can be incorporated in the floor pattern or finish, circles and squares provide the children with all sorts of games.

Likewise, circles on the walls, painted wickets, wendy houses, slides, small bench seats at different heights, can all be used to attract the child's interest and help him to co-ordinate his movements.

Anything which is specifically for adults only must be made clearly so by its design and position.

Cloakroom areas

Fittings here consist principally of arrangements for hanging coats and for changing shoes.

Coat pegs on rails are usual and these need to be at two different levels to allow for the differing reach of the children.

Spacing is wider than in ordinary schools, say about 600 mm (24 in) centre to centre with heights ranging between 1 m (3 ft 6 in) and 1.4 m (4 ft 6 in).

A sense of personal property and personal identity is helped by marking pegs, either by means of the child's name, a number, a colour or a symbol placed beside the peg. As these may change from time to time due to changes in the population of the school, it should be possible to change these peg marks in some way.

A bench seat is provided for changing shoes, with a bar or rack below it. Lockers are not usually needed.

Some of the children will need assistance; space standards should be generous and tight planning avoided.

Benches should preferably not be sited under rows of pegs or acrobatics and possible injury may result.

Mobile coat and shoe racks with a combined bench seat are often useful.

Toilets

Choice of fittings for these bears a certain relation to the factors considered in ordinary schools. Thus small W.C.s and low mounted wash-basins are provided for infants and a more normal size and mounting height for juniors and seniors.

Since the general feeling should be small in scale and bear as much affinity as possible with normal home life, there does not seem to be any great argument in favour of eccentric sizes or mounting heights, and the main point to observe in the design of an installation is that it should be as domestic as possible in feeling.

Teaching by use is an important matter in this area, as elsewhere, and a normal fitting used in a normal way is desirable. Ordinary low-level W.C. suites of simple pattern with standard plastic hinged seat and cover are therefore to be preferred. They may get broken occasionally, but that risk is far preferable to the risk of inculcating a hopelessly defeatist outlook through providing "armoured" break-proof W.C.s with concealed cisterns suitable in their detailing for a penitentiary or an old style asylum.

At all times the children need supervision and help but also a certain privacy, and even a certain reliance by staff and teachers on the child's own abilities, if they are to make progress and build confidence.

Wall mounted or wall bracketed W.C.s are easier for cleaning but this is virtually the only concession which need be made.

Likewise, large utility urinal slabs are not necessary, especially as they are not domestic in character. A small slab or even bowl urinals will often inculcate care and personal cleanliness. Of course, discreet attention should still be given to the design and detailing of the surrounding finishes. A deep continuous trough urinal mounted on the wall at normal bowl height has been found very successful.

Wash-basins should be in small groups rather than in long and forbidding ranges. As with other things, the children need to feel a certain sense of personal belonging. Many of them may prefer always to use a particular wash basin which they look on as their own.

Apart from washing the hands and face, the children often keep their toothbrushes and mugs in holders above the basins and these are labelled in large distinctive letters with their own names or symbols. This helps further in the sense of personal belonging. Ideally, a "personal" wash-basin for every child might be good, but in a building catering for sixty or eighty children this is not likely to be practical. At the same time, the placing of two or three toothbrush holders to each basin is feasible and gives an idea of the minimum number of basins required, and if these are arranged in small groups, the illusion of personal belonging is heightened.

It should be clear from this that grouping of pipework and economy of service runs are not the most important consideration when designing a building of this type.

Arrangements for holding soap should be simple and effective. The children are often clumsy and easily discouraged. If they are to learn simple things like the proper use of soap, the slippery lump must stay in its dish when put there.

Ordinary capstan head taps are preferable — once again on the ground that they are homely in character. They are also easily recognisable and their mode of operation is straightforward. New and patent types of head fitting should be avoided. Likewise, the use of concussive taps is not particularly to be recommended. The use of a single tap delivering ready-mixed hot water is not advised. It ignores the need for drinking water, the need for cold water for tooth brushing, and above all it fails completely to teach the child to handle normal equipment.

A splashback and mirror are needful adjuncts to a basin installation.

In practice, the amount of water which is run to waste through improper use will be no more than in a normal school and quite probably less. Basins should always have an overflow of course, in addition to a standard plug and waste. Hot and cold should be differentiated by coloured symbols.

Baths will be used in residential hostels and one or two baths are also provided in day centres. Mixing valves are useful in this situation, as the water is run by the staff.

In the case of baths in residential centres, the fittings are installed in a normal type of bathroom and require little comment. Both boys and girls living in residential hostels have achieved a certain basic proficiency in the everyday things of life and are generally able to bath themselves.

Children who need bathing by staff, however, require facilities which are different. The cause may be a physical disability or it may be a mental and/or emotional disturbance leading to non-cooperation and antisocial behaviour. Children at this level frequently foul themselves and need bathing. The problem can be acute and unpleasant, and facilities should be provided which are as easy as possible for the staff to use but which, at the same time, are pleasant and normal and in no way frightening to the children.

This is a very difficult installation and in practice such cleaning facilities are sometimes either rejected by the staff as unusable or are greatly disliked by the children and may even accentuate emotional disturbance.

A low height easily cleaned W.C. with a good flush and very quick refill should be provided, together with total bathing facility in close juxtaposition, with a flexible shower hose. Staff should not have to stoop too much in dealing with the child but the latter should not feel that he is on a sort of pedestal. Easy access on both sides of the bath is an asset especially in dealing with physically handicapped children, who may need lifting into the bath and who cannot easily change their position. Nevertheless, bathing and cleaning should be as ordinary as possible without any air of special ritual.

Plenty of clean, warm, dry towels will be needed, together with bin containers for fouled clothing which will be moved to the sluice room or laundry for washing.

There is likely to be a good deal of water splashing and the sides of the bath or vessel should be capable of retaining and retrieving it as far as possible.

A shower is not a satisfactory solution as it cannot be used for small, physically handicapped, or frightened children.

Bathing arrangements are likely to vary greatly as between one building and another according to staff preference and local needs. Where more than one bath is provided, it is a good plan to have at least two different heights. Although the baths themselves have low sides, they may need raising to enable staff to work efficiently. A useful idea is to have the floor at different heights at opposite sides of a free standing bath, which gives a very much improved versatility. Care should be taken when selecting baths to ensure a good horizontal area in cross-section. The child is likely to stand in the bath and unduly rounded cross-section is dangerous.

20. PART OF A SIX-BED DORMITORY BEDROOM AT A RESIDENTIAL HOSTEL.
The room is reasonably domestic in scale and the decor is pleasant but the bed areas are not
sufficiently individual. The mirrors are not well placed and the fitted furniture is needlessly
elaborate.

A sluice room should adjoin the toilet and bath area in buildings for young children and for very disturbed or difficult children. This is equipped with a sluice and a deep sink.

Bedrooms

The term "bedroom" is preferable to "dormitory" as the rooms only accommodate a small number of children.

Furniture is movable but each bed should have its own locker and hanging space. For older children a small single wardrobe is desirable. Ideally, each bed should be surrounded by its own little area of personal influence. A locker, a bedside shelf, a small rug can all help to achieve this.

Lounges

These are usually divided into two distinct areas or even two rooms, one large and noisy and the other smaller and for quieter pursuits. In practice it is difficult to separate the two, but changes in the finishes and furnishings can help.

Serviceable sitting-room furniture is required and the chairs should never line the walls, but should be arranged in sociable groups.

The aim is to reproduce normality. Some lounges even provide an open fireplace (usually with a convector electric fire) and this focal point actually encourages some children to sit round and engage in quiet activities.

LEISURE

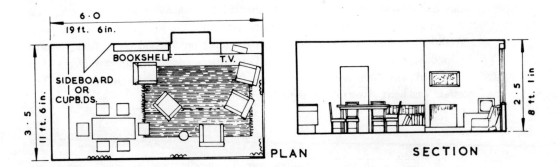

PLAN   SECTION

Typical lounge/sitting room layout for chalet/bungalow type of residence usually 6/9 children ·
Size and furnishings very similar to ordinary domestic layout · Used for sitting, reading, watching
T.V., quiet hobbies and activities · Also for supper, drinks, and snacks · Sometimes for meals ·
Such sitting rooms are sometimes paired with a central link kitchen · Furnishings should be
reasonably varied

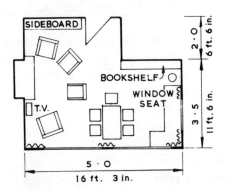

PLAN

Alternative layout still small and domestic in scale
but with alternative 'quiet withdrawal' areas and a
modest amount of open space

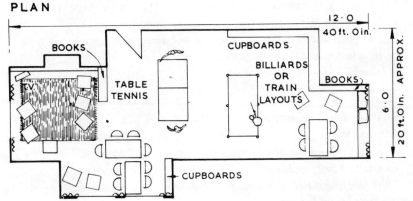

PLAN

Leisure layout for larger group of up to 20/30
children · Active games incorporated but as many
'retiring' corners and quiet sitting areas as possible
simulating domestic living · Room environment ·
Avoid using standardised furnishings or lining the
walls with chairs as these give an undesirable
institutional look

NOTE: Dimensions should be regarded
only as an approximate guide to space
standards

Fig. 24

105

H

Television is usually provided. Book shelves and cupboards will be required.

The writer was interested to note that at a residential hostel where several dayrooms were provided *en suite*, the children always seemed to favour one particular room. It had four separate doors, a built in fireplace with a panel electric fire suitably protected, a carpet square on a wood block floor, normal windows, two or three Parker Knoll armchairs and some upright chairs. The colour scheme was predominantly light beige and the room faced south. The effect was light, cheerful but entirely unremarkable.

Door design

The design of doors requires special consideration. In day centres and residential centres there is not a high degree of security and very few doors are locked. For special care, however, it may be needful to keep doors locked, at any rate for the more disturbed cases, as some of them are given to wandering or even escapism.

For general purposes a 850 mm (2 ft 9 in) single door is sufficient. Door checks and closers may lead to accidents and there have been many cases of trapped fingers.

Ordinary lever handle furniture is easy to operate and is perhaps the best to use, mounting height being normal domestic height. Mortice locks are used as only the possessor of the key can operate them. Cylinder latches often cause unexpected problems and should not be used.

A glass observation panel is provided in doors for normal use. Glass in lower panels however, serves no purpose and gets broken, often by objects carried by children. In one or two extreme cases it has even caused injury.

Wider doors or double doors are needed for Special Care Units involving cot or wheelchair cases. Doors for toilets are solid and the entrance doors to toilet areas are often labelled "Gentlemen" and "Ladies" a little touch which helps children to become familiar with everyday situations.

For very young children, doors to W.C.s are non-locking and only three feet or four feet high to permit staff control.

Windows

These must be easy to operate but safe in use. Pivot windows are not very safe and the projection they form when open is dangerous.

A vertical sliding type of window seems to be most effective. If the lower part opens, however, children climb onto cills and cupboard tops and may fall out. Thus any permitted opening at a low level should be narrow or else protected (preferably the former) and main opening areas should be at a higher level.

Windows which commence at floor level are misleading and dangerous.

Horizontal sliding windows present the same problems as vertical sliding windows, but in an accentuated form. Louvred windows provide good ventilation and are worth consideration.

CHAPTER 7

Colour, pattern and texture in environment

Colour, pattern and texture play a tremendously important part in forming the total environment, a part out of all proportion to the ease with which they can be varied. Very often the designer fails to realise this and devises the decor without any regard for its positive value.

Choice of colour and choice of pattern can influence the child in many ways. At one extreme it is possible to produce violent and disturbing effects—at the other it is possible to produce an environment which is completely negative. At various points between these two extremes lie the most obvious and desirable conditions—those in which a relaxed and happy atmosphere has been created overall and in which there is sufficient brightness and interest to attract the child and to stimulate thought or activity.

A certain amount of research has been done in this field though the results do not appear to be widely known or extended to practical applications in the field of the built environment. Some researchers have gone as far as to experiment with self-applied drugs in order to try and create the visual disturbance and distortion of the senses which may occur in disturbed children.

It is hard to say how valid or useful such experimentation may prove to be. At the same time the designer must always design with the root problem in mind. In effect he must imagine himself somewhat smaller, perhaps only three feet high; he must forget his adult experience and his adult confidence, and he must try and get behind the fears and uncertainties, often irrational, of a child. Such a need poses the utmost difficulties and there is a limit to what can be achieved in this direction. It may be foolish to try and design the buildings or even the interiors as a child would design, but this does not remove the need to design as a sympathetic, understanding and, above all, imaginative adult, able to share fears and to smooth them away.

In designing, the interior should be tested and assessed from every possible angle. Long vistas formed by the perspective of a corridor have already been mentioned—this perspective is heightened if one views it from a lesser height. Similarly a vanishing perspective can be formed by parallel joints in floor boards

21. HOUNSLOW CENTRE
Two photographs which illustrate the difference in visual impression caused by viewing a building or feature firstly from normal adult height and secondly from the height of a small child.
Architect: G. A. Trevett, A.R.I.B.A., Borough Architect, London Borough of Hounslow.

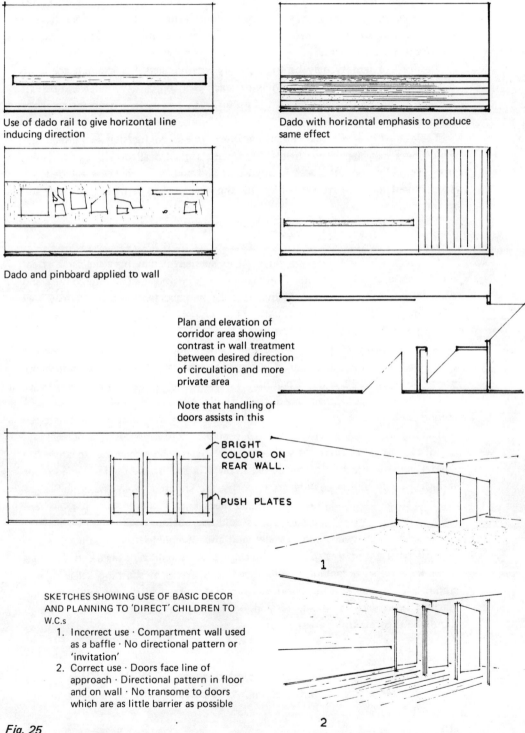

Use of dado rail to give horizontal line inducing direction

Dado with horizontal emphasis to produce same effect

Dado and pinboard applied to wall

Plan and elevation of corridor area showing contrast in wall treatment between desired direction of circulation and more private area

Note that handling of doors assists in this

BRIGHT COLOUR ON REAR WALL.

PUSH PLATES

1

SKETCHES SHOWING USE OF BASIC DECOR AND PLANNING TO 'DIRECT' CHILDREN TO W.C.s

1. Incorrect use · Compartment wall used as a baffle · No directional pattern or 'invitation'

2. Correct use · Doors face line of approach · Directional pattern in floor and on wall · No transome to doors which are as little barrier as possible

2

Fig. 25

which could be frighteningly large to a child. A row of identical doors, all closed and all solid, so that everything beyond them is unknown, could have a traumatic effect.

Although this aspect may seem exaggerated it should be remembered that a proportion of the children suffer perceptual disturbance. They may have a private world of their own in which values are different and in which appearances are different.

Reality and fantasy may be frighteningly intermingled. For example there are disturbed children for whom a chimney stack is a source of wonder and delight but for whom the open rear of a furniture van has sufficient horror to make them scream with fear.

These are extreme cases and the designer who could forestall every such fear would be a magician. Nevertheless, he can do a great deal to help. For instance, the clear definition of spaces is important and ambiguity must be avoided. An environment must be created which has the attributes of harmony, of peace and of interest.

Colour

Colour can be used in many ways. At its simplest it may have the same effect on the child as on the adult. The well-known principle that strong colours and dark colours "advance" towards the beholder and shorten the distance may well affect the spatial aspect of the interior. Likewise, effects of space and perhaps of sunlight may be produced by light colours.

A combination of light colours and dark colours may be used to give a directional emphasis to space. Colour contrasts may be so strong in close juxtaposition as to be actually painful.

It has often been maintained that people respond differently to different colours and there may well be scope for research in this field. For example red and orange are commonly believed to produce more activity than normal and green to have a soothing effect, whilst yellow has been claimed to stimulate mental activity. Black is often looked upon as a sad or even a fearsome colour though a study of the colours preferred by the children when "painting" might produce some interesting results. Red and black both figure prominently, perhaps because they are strong and have a very bold and obvious covering power.

Consultation between the designer and the psychologist may be well worth while if both are interested in the subject. Colour should be considered as an aid to establishing an acceptable environment, as a means of soothing, cheering and stimulating. It may also be considered as a motivational force. For example some teachers have decided views, formed on experience, about the colours which should be used for toilet areas.

Pattern

Pattern, likewise, can be used to produce a calculated effect. Once again a sense of direction may be achieved, either by pattern on the walls or by pattern

PATTERN

CEILINGS, WALLS, AND FLOORS

General effect should be light and permit flexibility in room arrangement · Avoid fixed focal points unless these serve a special purpose.

Strong directional emphasis may be used for specific purposes.

Example of ceiling pattern and wall feature helping circulation flow.

Patterns on walls and floor used as 'reminder' or 'persuader'.

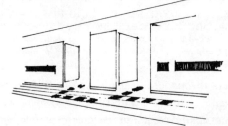

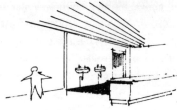

Change of pattern used to suggest change of activity. '
Ceiling pattern 'leads in' to the space.

Within a general activity area or space where children remain, the pattern can 'encircle' the group provided it is not oppressive.

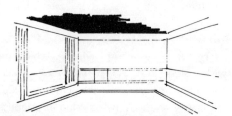

Floors can be patterned to help movement and co-ordination.
Lino or tiles form:

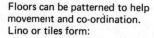

Straight lines;

Stepping stones;

Circular islands;

Hop-scotch and other games patterns.

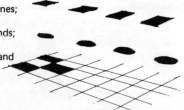

Floor patterns can be used to lead to an object.

Ceilings should not have heavy repetitive patterns.

Fig. 26

111

22. THE ROYAL SEA BATHING HOSPITAL, MARGATE
The playroom of the children's ward for which the Design Department of Marley, Sevenoaks produced this appealing motif. The floor was of HD vinyl tiles and seven colours were used for the donkey motif. *(Courtesy, Hospital Management Committee).*

on the floor or ceiling. Some children respond more readily to shape than to colour. Interest and stimulation may be achieved by pattern effects but this possibility must not be over-exploited and above all the children must not be bewildered by clever trick effects. Op-art decoration might arouse interest on a variable or mobile panel but would not be particularly desirable as permanent decor to a classroom or lounge wall. Shape and pattern can be used to establish an effect of order, harmony, and might also be used as a corrective and a stimulus.

Texture

Texture is a further adjunct which might be used to good effect combined with colour and shape. The tactile feel of an object or surface is often of absorbing interest to the children. Constant touching will help to induce familiarity and may be of value in establishing a feeling of security.

Thus the child may like to touch the furniture or the walls or features on the walls. He may take pleasure in playing "stepping stone" games on floor tiles or on lino.

Perhaps these actions will seem futile to the adult practising designer but any positive interest or activity may present a chance which might be turned to advantage. At the very least it may have a therapeutic effect. At the best it could afford an opportunity of "getting through" to a difficult child, where ordinary things have failed.

To a certain extent a child may make his or her own surroundings within the designed environment. Somewhere within most children there is an urge to make their own environment, often rather messy and disorganised to adult eyes but possessing its own form and its own order. Children like to make their own corners with their own personal things, they are often intrigued by such things as mobiles and play-sculpture, even a piece of wood may have a fascination. The designer would do well to learn from these preferences.

CHAPTER 8

Physically handicapped children

Types of handicap

A relatively small proportion of mentally handicapped children are also physically handicapped. For these children a full cure is very unlikely within the present extent of knowledge, except, perhaps, in cases of physical handicap through actual physical injury.

The commonest case is that of the spastic child — about whom much has already been written. Many of the children will develop through the growth of their own latent abilities. Others suffer under a wide variety of physical disabilities including deformation of many kinds, and whilst their numbers are mercifully small their case is pathetic in the extreme. Some are little more than vegetables. Most of these extremes cases will be in residential hospital care.

Those with a more manageable physical handicap will probably be in day care and it is these children with which this chapter is concerned.

They can be divided into:

a Ambulant physical handicap cases.

b Semi-ambulant wheelchair cases.

c Non-ambulant chair and cot cases. (The number in day care in this group is small)

Day care is normally provided in the form of a Special Unit either attached to a Junior Training School or functioning as a separate unit. Special Units, as currently conceived, provide not only for mental/physical handicap but also for mental/behavioural handicap and this problem clearly needs more thought than it has received so far from the authorities.

Staff who are busy dealing with wheelchair cases cannot help behavioural cases adequately at the same time. The level of intelligence and ability also varies quite alarmingly and there is a very strong argument for re-thinking the role and the planning of the Special Unit, which should certainly not be a dumping ground for the difficult cases and misfits.

Physically handicapped children travel either in a minibus with wide rear doors or by ambulance.

As far as possible their day is spent in the same type of activities as those of the Junior Training School though on a lower and less consistent level. The fact that there will be more difficulty and less success in their training and education is due to both the additional physical handicap and, often, to resulting emotional problems.

Planning needs—doors and thresholds

If a special unit is provided for physically handicapped cases as part of a larger group of buildings, this will almost certainly have a separate entrance.

Entrances for wheelchair cases should be suitably wide. An arrangement permitting the approach of chairs at 90° rather than at an oblique angle, and the effect of obstructions, including the edge of the open door and the projection of door furniture, should be studied. A minimum width of 850 mm (2 ft 9 in) for a single door is advisable. Double doors should be detailed with care as it does not necessarily follow that staff will automatically use both doors if they think this can be avoided.

The "handing" of doors should not mask the room as in normal buildings, as this makes access more difficult.

Swing doors are easier to operate than sliding doors where children are concerned, and it is an advantage in entrances and corridors if the doors swing in both directions. Doors to "classrooms" and other rooms at 90° to the line of travel can only swing both ways if they are recessed in order to avoid a dangerous swing into other circulation space. Door closers should only be used with great care.

Steps should be avoided, and where a change in floor level occurs, as at entrances from outside, a ramp is preferable. Combination of ramp and shallow steps for different types of disability should be used with great caution, and a physical barrier between the two is advisable. A hand-rail beside ramps is required, as much for the benefit of supervision staff as for the children.

Thresholds should be unobstructed or have a compressible rubber strip type of threshold bar.

Doors should have a glazed observation panel—not too low—and should be provided with a generous depth of kicking plate. Easy action door fastenings are needed where the children are able to move from room to room. Lever handles are good for this purpose or even push plates and a roller ball catch. Where security is needed the handles and lock will require to be at a higher level. Corners of openings and the lower part of walls need protection from damage by sticks and foot-rests. A high skirting or hard wearing dado is advisable.

Toilets

Toilet arrangements need particular care. W.C.s should provide ample space at the side since staff will almost certainly need to render assistance. W.C. compartments should be 1,400 mm (4 ft 6 in) wide and provided with two support rails to assist in different types of physical disability. A wide outward opening door may be provided and in some instances privacy is afforded by placing W.C.s back-to-back with wing walls without any other form of enclosure. A washbasin is often provided beside the W.C. Fittings mounted at two or even three different levels are an asset. Urinals should be large trough-type fittings preferably raised above floor level. The comments already made concerning baths apply equally. Bathing facilities are used to a much greater extent since there is likely to be far greater incontinence.

Baths and sluices

Shallow baths not more than 350 mm (14 in) or 400 mm (15 in) deep are needed and grip rails are required.

A short hip bath is particularly useful for the purpose though it does not provide the therapeutic value of relaxing at full length in warm water which is sometimes beneficial for disturbed cases.

A difference in floor level at opposite sides of the bath (which is itself free-standing) is an asset to the staff during the process of bathing children.

Simple lifting devices may be needed for some of the severely handicapped children. Designers must always remember however that facilities should be as ordinary as possible and great care must be taken not to turn bathing into a ritual or to frighten or disturb the children in any way by the nature of the facilities.

A sluice room is needed and may be combined with bathing facilities, though a minor degree of separation may be better psychologically.

A complete installation for dealing with combined incontinence and physical handicap should include a W.C., a sluice and sink, containers for fouled clothing and a bath with shower attachment. Laundry facilities are equally important and take the form of a small laundry room with a heavy-duty washer, spin-dryer, and drying and ironing facilities.

Classrooms

The layout and fitting of "classrooms" or day rooms is conditioned to some extent by physical handicap. Ambulant children using sticks or crutches, and wheelchair cases, require more space in which to manoeuvre than children who are able to walk and move normally. The layout of furniture and fittings should be designed with this requirement in mind.

Support rails fixed to the walls, especially near doors and windows, are very useful.

Training and education of mentally handicapped children are commonly regarded as difficult and the difficulties are increased when physical handicap also exists. An important part of their training is likely to be instruction and help in movement and the performance of physical tasks. Various types of grip rail, wall bars and floor mounted bars may be of help in this. Likewise the attachment of lifting devices to the ceiling may be necessary and a grid of suitably positioned ceiling fixings is required. Ceilings should not consist of light suspended tiles but should afford firm fixings at all points.

Cupboards, lockers and work benches should be designed so that children can use them whilst seated in wheelchairs. Care must be taken that adequate knee space is provided.

Furniture must be heavier and more substantial than is normally the case in buildings where children are not physically handicapped.

Access is needed direct from classrooms to sheltered outdoor play areas and the comments already made concerning doors and thresholds apply here.

Particular care must be taken to provide shelter from both cold and strong direct sun.

Dining areas

Dining areas require the same care with the design and layout of tables. A greater degree of staff assistance is needed and some of the children will require not only serving but also feeding.

Some cases may be under drug treatment and there will be others who do not move about much. Provision should be made for the children to rest after lunch for a short period, though not all of them will do so. Some will rest in chairs or wheelchairs but cots and small camp beds will also be required.

Good storage facilities are required, providing not only for the usual materials and equipment, but also for walking and lifting aids and for a small number of wheelchairs. The latter may conveniently be stored near the entrance to the building.

EPILOGUE

The Present and the Future

The entire question of care (and therefore of buildings) for mentally handicapped children is currently undergoing change. More is being done and more consideration is being given to the problem than ever before. This alone, however, is far from being enough.

Although money is being spent on buildings and on staff it must be used to the fullest possible advantage. Educationally there is scope for improvement.

Organisationally, much more could be done, especially in the linkage between the various possible facilities for children of different ages and abilities. Medically there are enormous advances yet to be made. The experts in these various fields are the only people who can suggest a line of advance.

Architecturally there is undoubtedly great room for improvement. There has not been a sufficiently close liasion between the architect as designer and those who will direct, administer, and use the buildings. There has been insufficient breadth of vision and depth of imagination. Especially, there has not been a sufficient assessment and re-appraisal of existing buildings and existing facilities.

There is a very strong case for systematic re-appraisal of planning and design. This can be gained by examination of existing buildings but more especially by a careful study of the activities carried on within them and by a careful analysis of these activities. Finally, there is a need for tactful experiment. The need for flexibility in the spatial division, fitting and use of the buildings has already been stressed. Experiment is still needed in many directions.

Is a rectangular room formation best? Would an informal, irregular arrangement be better? Should the ceiling be high or low, flat or inclined? Do colours always have the same effects and at all times?

So many questions remain to be answered and almost nothing is known with any certainty. The only way in which designers and teachers alike can gain more knowledge and more accurate knowledge of needs is by means of methodical experiment.

References

BAYES, KENNETH—"The therapeutic effect of environment on emotionally disturbed and mentally subnormal Children". Kaufman International Design Award Study, 1964-6.

BERENSON, BERTRAM—*Architecture for Exceptional Children.* University of Michigan. Arch. Res. Conference, 1965.

BETTELHEIM, BRUNO—"Love is not enough". Macmillan, New York, 1950. *Truants from life.* The Free Press, Glencoe, Illinois, 1955.

BIRREN, FABER—*Colour, Form and Space.* Reinhold, New York, 1961.

BROWN, R. I.—"Problems of attention in the education and training of the subnormal". Research Unit, Institute of Education, Bristol.

BURN, MICHAEL—*Mr. Lywards Answer.* Hamish Hamilton, London, 1964.

CLARKE, A. M. and A. D. B.—Mental Deficiency: The Changing Outlook, Methuen, London, 1966.

CURZON, WINIFRED M.—"Training of Mentally Handicapped Children in Day Centres". *Development Medicine & Child Neurology* Vol. 4 No. 5.

EDUCATION AND SCIENCE—Dept. of—Building Bulletin No. 27, 1965. Boarding Schools for Maladjusted Children.

GIBSON, JAMES J.—Perception of the Visual World. Allen & Unwin, London. Houghton Miflin, Boston, 1950.

GOLDSMITH, SELWYN—*Designing for the Disabled.* Royal Institute of British Architects, 1967.

GREGORY, R. L.—*Eye and Brain.* Weidenfeld and Nicholson, London, 1966.

GUNZBURG, ANNA—"Architecture for Social Rehabilitation". *Journal of Mental Subnormality.* Dec. 1967, Vol. XIII/2, **25**, p.p. 84-87.

GUNZBURG, ANNA—"Sensory Experiences in the Architecture for the Mentally Subnormal Child". *Journal of Mental Subnormality.* June 1968, Vol. XIV/1, **26**, p.p 57-58

HAYS, PETER—*New Horizons in Psychiatry.* Penguin, Harmondsworth, 1964.

IZUMI, K—"Psychological Phenomena and Building Design". Building Research, July/August 9-11, 1965.

KOENIG, K.—*The Handicapped Child*—New Knowledge Books, East Grinstead, 1954.

LONDON SCHOOL OF HYGIENE AND TROPICAL MEDICINE—*A Study of the Mentally Handicapped Child.* Study Group 1961/2—National Society for Mentally Handicapped Children.

NATIONAL SOCIETY FOR METALLY HANDICAPPED CHILDREN—*The Psychotic Child,* 1961.

O'CONNOR & HERMELIN—*Speech and Thought in Severe Subnormality.* Pergamon Press, Oxford, 1963.

TIZARD, J.—*Community Services for the Mentally Handicapped.* O.U.P. London, 1964.

TIZARD, J.—"Some Problems of Management of Young Mentally Handicapped Children".—A paper.

VERNON, M. D.—The *Psychology of Perception*—Penguin Books, Harmondsworth, 1962.

WING, LORNA—*Autistic Children.* National Association for Mental Health, London.

WORLD HEALTH ORGANISATION—*The Mentally Subnormal Child.* Geneva, 1954.

WORLD HEALTH ORGANISATION—*Psychiatric Services and Architecture.* Geneva, 1959.

ZEAMAN and HOUSE—"The role of attention in retardate discrimination learning". Chapter 5. *Handbook of Mental Deficiency*—McGraw-Hill, New York.

Index *Italic figures indicate illustrations*